II

Behind the Dress

One woman's life in a religious cult and the healing that came much later

By
Christine Faour

Copyright © Christine Faour 2022

All rights reserved. No part of this publication may be reproduced, stored in a retrieval system, or transmitted in any form or by any means, electronic, mechanical, photocopying, recording, or otherwise without the prior permission of the author.

Cover design by Hellhag Productions

ISBN 978-0-9878306-1-6

Christine Faour
Coldbrook, Nova Scotia
Canada
www.anourishedlife.ca

Hello and thank you for picking up my book. I hope you will be blessed by reading it and that you will see that even when the worst happens, change for the better is possible if you are able to be courageous.

My hope for you is that you will find comfort from my experiences and come to the realization that we are not alone. We never were alone, even though we thought we were. Since this book has been published, I have had numerous people come to me and say things like,

"Although I wasn't in a cult, I can relate very well to what you wrote about ATI and your experiences. My church was something like that but not as extreme."

"I found comfort from your book because I also was released from an abusive marriage and the feelings of unworthiness that you speak about."

"I was raised in ATI and reading your book helped me to understand why my parents made us do the things we did."

If you have any comments, queries, or questions, I can be reached at christinefaour@gmail.com. I would also be willing to speak to your group about my experiences.

"In this candidly written book Christine Faour takes the reader through her involvement in a religious cult and the changes it made in her life, especially her self-perception. Once out of the cult and recognizing it for what it was, she faced the challenge of once again becoming fully herself. The book makes it very clear that it may be easier to accept a new belief system that has been skillfully presented than it is to shed it once a decision has been made to leave the group espousing it. She shares stories of events and daily life as well as how she saw them at the time and as well as her new understanding of them now. Christine's experience has relevance to other instances of indoctrination in both process and outcome. As serious as the topic is, the book is written with humor and a level of detail that make it very readable."

Eloise Comeau Murray Professor Emerita, University of Alberta

"This first-person account of a Canadian woman's life in an American Christian cult as a wife and mother is compelling and readable. It is poignant in addressing the author's mental and physical journey into, during, and following the cult years.

There are moments of empowerment, self-knowledge, and self-acceptance, which make for an enjoyable read."

Bruce Bishop, author, *Unconventional Daughters,* and *Uncommon Sons*

Dedication

This memoir is dedicated to all the women, be they wives, mothers, daughters, or grandmothers, who have survived a cult, but especially the cult that was The Advanced Training Institute

Author's Note

This is a work of nonfiction, a real-life account of my past in ATI as I remember it and how I felt during that time. It relies mostly on my memories of people and places. There are some recollections that may not fit with other peoples' perception, but this is, after all, my story and my perceptions and thoughts on the life we lived. To protect the people written about in this memoir, I have changed all their names except my present husband Dave, and my own name. Also, our home address in St. Eustache has been changed.

Table of Contents

1. Armageddon
2. Come Here and I'll Tell You
3. Meeting the Guy: Meant to Be?
4. Marriage and a Suitcase
5. Getting Into the Program
6. What is it About Suitcases?
7. Homeschooling in ATI
8. Weird, Peculiar or Just Plain Stupid
9. One Day I Woke Up Happy
10. Can I have a Nervous Breakdown Now?
11. The Proverbs 31 Woman
12. Honey, Have You Felt the Pain?
13. The Incredible Self-effacing Woman
14. I'm Too Holy for My Church
15. Guilt and Gas Fireplaces
16. Getting Through the Daze
17. A Total Cleanout
18. Tears And Some Good Advice
19. Moving Day
20. Divorce Fudge
21. The Day I Forgot My Name
22. It Must Be God's Will
23. Dating Sites
24. Letters to Jamie on the Christian Café

25.	First Soulful, Romantic Encounter
26.	The Day My Heart Broke
27.	Depressed – Who, Me?
28.	Single Again
29.	Lavender Saved Me
30.	I had Forgotten Who I Was
31.	How I Met My New Husband
32.	When the Time is Right
33.	A New Life in Nova Scotia
34.	A Paddle of Shame
35.	Finding Out I Was in a Cult
36.	The Dawning of Understanding
37.	I Can See Clearly Now
38.	Three Questions
39.	Out of the Ashes, Beauty Will Rise

Book club discussion questions

Appendix

Afterword

1
Armageddon

For all the world, it was just a normal October day in St. Eustache, Quebec as I made my way up Boulevard Arthur Sauvé to stop at la Banque Royale. Inside the building, men and women were going about their business with their attaché cases in hand. They all looked like they had important things to do as their heels clicked on shining marble floors and their perfectly coiffed hair bouncing in time with each step. To them, I was just another person going to the bank to conduct my business on a sunny Tuesday in October. But on that day, I didn't feel like just any other person. I felt that I was doing something illicit. But I wasn't.

With heart pounding, I arrived at the bank doors. I furtively looked around as I approached the teller, hoping she couldn't notice the smell. Her pleasant smile was almost too much for me because I didn't think I deserved to be smiled at. I asked her if I could see someone in an enclosed room because I had a very large amount of cash to deposit. I tried to keep my voice and hands from shaking, I was so overcome with fear and dread of what was happening to my life. I'm not sure what I was afraid of at that point- that someone would take my money; that He (with a capital H) would arrive at the bank and catch me? I don't know, but I really felt as if I was doing something wrong. At that point only I knew what was in the bulging purse at my side. Just for a little while longer, it was my secret, and I could have turned and left at any time. But I dutifully followed two other bank officials, and when we got into an office, they watched in amazement as I emptied my large purse onto the table, and the tiny room filled with the stench of mildew. I knew they were not supposed to express judgement in any way, but I could see their minds going in overdrive at the sight of all that smelly money. Stinky, dirty money. And then they told me they were obliged to ask me where I got it from and what was I planning to do with it. In a split second, many answers came to mind, but the truth was probably going to be the only answer that might be believed.

There was a little machine on a side table that looked strangely familiar. I wondered why they had a card shuffler at a bank. But no, it was for counting money. As they gingerly put the bills into that machine to be counted, and over the clackety clack of its operation, I told them my story of Y2K and the combination safe embedded in the basement floor of our home. I finished by telling them that now, since Y2K was no longer a threat, I had decided to deposit the money. Nervously trying to chat them up, I asked if there had been anyone else in my situation and they assured me that no, there hadn't been.

But the thing was, the true story was just crazy enough that they believed me. After all the paperwork was done, they opened a new account in my name only. I went home that day with not only an empty purse and a new bank account but also with a bit of newfound independence. As I exited the bank with my head held high and only a shred of dignity left, I could imagine them snickering in French at the lunatic Christian that had just made their day.

There was a whole series of events that brought me to that day at la Banque Royale in St. Eustache, Quebec. I had almost forgotten that very eventful day. But a sometimes a little reminder can bring back things forgotten.

It's interesting how a present-day event can bring up memories from the past, with all their vivid emotions, colour and detail. It happens to me all the time that something from my years in the cult will intrude into the life I'm living now. They are memories that float by my consciousness, and it still astounds me that I lived such a life. For example, I recently sold my car for $9000, and the person who bought it paid me with 90 one hundred-dollar bills. He thought it was a cool thing to do.

While we sat at my kitchen table and filled out the registration forms, it was a thrill for me to see the stack of bills piled up on the table, all brand new. They even smelled new. I asked the guy if the bank people wanted to know why he needed $9000 in one hundred-dollar bills. As he nodded, saying that he told them it was none of their business, I was brought back to a time sixteen years prior when I was asked the same question as I sat in a banker's office with a purse full of twenty-dollar bills.

Back in my cult days, there was a scripture verse that we often quoted when we realized we were incredibly different from everyone else. It was from a version of the bible that read like this: "But you are a chosen generation, a royal priesthood, a peculiar people…" and on it went. We took that verse as our own and used it to explain to the children why we were so different from everyone else. We didn't see the term, 'peculiar people' as a criticism but rather as a badge of honor, in that we were God's cream of the crop. But the problem was that we were getting more and more peculiar every day. We had been homeschooling for 10 years, eating vegan for three years, we dressed differently from everyone else, and we were house churching under the guidance of another house church in Vermont because the churches in the area weren't holy enough for us.

In the summer of 1999, our sister house church in Vermont started talking to us about Y2K and about how we needed to get ready because the 'millennium bug' was coming. As the year 2000 approached, many people believed that the computer systems would not interpret the "00" correctly, therefore causing a major glitch in the system.

There would be no food, no money and in general there would be mayhem at the turn of the century when all the computers in the land would collapse as the year turned from 1999 to 2000. It would be a major event that would affect the whole world. Food supply would be affected as well as clean water, gas, money and every aspect of life that was in some way connected to the internet. Their solution, and they urged us to do the same, was to stockpile food, money, clothing, and ammunition for the guns that would help them guard it all. They built root cellars. They bought thousands of dollars' worth of prepackaged food for the coming disaster. We bought some, but it didn't look so great. It was dehydrated meals and all you had to do was to add water. In Montreal, no one else was preparing, that we knew of.

Since we lived in Canada and we couldn't keep guns and ammunition, because that would make us outlaws in addition to the rest of our peculiarities, we decided to stockpile food, water, and money. We bought a year's supply of wheat and a hand grinder so that we could grind the wheat (by hand because there would be no power) to make bread, mountains of canned food, dry food, and tons of toilet paper. We procured a couple of fifty-gallon drums to fill with water by the end of the year. I had a hard time to imagine how all this difficulty would come to pass as we lived in a wonderful agricultural belt in Quebec, and the fresh food grown close by would continue to grow, wouldn't it? And I asked time and again, if we were the only people with food and water, wouldn't we share it with the neighbors? I guess not; that's why our American friends had stockpiled guns and ammunition.

And the piece de resistance? We lifted the carpet in a basement closet, drilled away at the concrete underneath, and sank a safe into the hole for hiding our money. My husband mixed up a bag of cement to surround it with, so that the safe could never be removed. Once it was embedded into the floor, we started to put money into it. Every week we added to our stash until we had $30 000 in 20-dollar bills, all counted out and in a Tupperware container in that safe. We made a very careful combination for the lock: our three sons' birthdays in descending order. Genius, right? And it was supposed to be a secret.

Our neighbors knew we were strange, but really, they had no idea of just how weird we were. Maybe that was a good thing.

That Christmas of 1999, we celebrated with the other members of our house church, what we thought would be the last Christmas as we knew it. We rang in the new year with computers open to see what would happen. Would the lights go out? Would planes fall out of the sky? With bated breath we surrounded the computer screen and waited. We shouted out the countdown. Midnight came. Midnight went. And nothing happened. We could hear fireworks in the distance as normal people celebrated the turn of the century. We looked at each other in what could be described as relief, but somehow dismay that we had been duped and had spent all that time and money preparing for the non-existent Armageddon.

The turn of the century arrived, and life went on. It was all a big hoax, and we were feeling a little foolish. And now we had all that dehydrated food to eat. Most of it went in the garbage because some tasted like cardboard and the rest like dog food. We emptied the 50-gallon drums in the bedrooms by siphoning the water through a tube out the window, and then we quietly sold the drums. We slowly ate the canned and packaged food, used the toilet paper, and went back to normal living, at least what was normal for our peculiar family. The last of the bags of organic wheat that we stockpiled still hadn't been used up fifteen years later.

But the $30 000 in twenty-dollar bills sat untouched, in the freezer bags, in the Tupperware container, in the safe embedded in the concrete under the carpet, in the closet in the basement of the house on 247 Rue Landry. So, in 2004, when my husband decided he was leaving me and the children to be with another woman, I figured this crazy life was about to change.

The first thing I did was to gather the necessary papers to bring to the lawyer. I needed legal help, and ready money. I didn't know how long our joint bank accounts would be available to me, and I never had a bank account of my own, not since I was married. I figured the money in the safe was as good as any to start a new life with, so I got it out of there while I still could. The bills, even though they were in plastic bags and then in a Tupperware container, were mildewed and they stank. This was after only five years of storage. The smell was really overpowering but it was also real money that now needed to go to the bank. I stuffed all the bills into my largest purse and the next day, headed to the bank to open a new account for my new life. I felt kind of stupid with a purse full of mildewed money, and I was an emotional wreck. Twenty-one years was a long time to have been married, and now it was ending.

The house on 247 Rue Landry housed my ex and his partner for a few years after our divorce, and then it was sold to a single mom whose son was best friends with my son. After we moved to Nova Scotia, he made many trips back to the house to spend summers with his friend. The safe is still there under the carpet in the basement and my youngest son showed the new owners not only that it was there but also how to open it. As far as I know, the combination is the same as when I set it back in 1999. It seems kind of ironic that he spent much of his growing up years in the same house he was born in.

****

This is my story of living in a fundamentalist cult for 21 years, and not understanding that it was a cult until I was ten years out of it. The fallout of the false teachings in the cult continue to affect me to this day. My story is for anyone who has been overly influenced by 'Christian principles' to the point they have lost themselves in submission and obedience. During those cult years I couldn't make a decision on my own, and to question what we were being asked to do was not allowed. I was constantly unsure of myself, and my self-confidence was in the gutter because I could never live up to the standards that were imposed on me. It's also the story of how I lost the essence of who I was and became a clone of every other wife and mother in the cult that was The Advanced Training Institute (ATI). We were taught how to dress, what to eat, how to behave, that we should smile all the time, how to raise our children and when to have sex.

When I met my husband, I was 30 years old and anxious to get on with my life; to settle down and start a family. I was a woman whose childhood and Catholic upbringing in Newfoundland probably set the stage for following the rules, gender roles and obedience that the cult of ATI required. My schooling, right through High School was under the direction of the Presentation Sisters who were probably missing some important ingredient for becoming complete and competent citizens. It was an all-girls school, so the important socialization with the opposite sex was nonexistent.

      Being raised in Corner Brook, Newfoundland, I was quite isolated from the rest of the world. For example, I tasted my first fresh mushroom when I was a young adult, corn on the cob came most often from a can; cherries were candied or came in a bottle, and apricots were dried and came in a bag. When I left Newfoundland, I tasted the fresh food that was seldom available on the island. Ninety miles of water cut us off from the rest of the world. I'm almost ashamed to admit it, but I first heard about the Vietnam war when I started university at St FXU in Antigonish, Nova Scotia.

2

Come Here and I'll Tell You

I was at an end of year gathering at a restaurant for my social group. About forty of us were seated in a room apart at the Port Pub in Port Williams, Nova Scotia. The trees swayed in the breeze outside our window as the Cornwallis River made its way into the Minas Basin, setting the scene for a fun time. Good food and friends added to the tantalizing atmosphere. We were waiting for our appetizers when I found myself the center of attention as I related my story to a rapt entourage about how I made and sold fudge to pay for my divorce a few years earlier. As much as it was a dark period of my life back then, we all had a great laugh about my fudge selling and how it is now known as Divorce Fudge. I had been selling it every year since then, and the label actually says, Divorce Fudge. People loved it. They thought I was amazing. I didn't feel terribly amazing, even many years later, but my friends loved my story. I think that was the first time I realized that I had anything to say that people would listen to.

A couple of years later, I realized that I had been in a cult. All 21 years of my first marriage, homeschooling my three sons in the confines and rules of the Advanced Training Institute of America, known as ATI had been spent in a cult. Who, me? How could I have been in a cult and not have known?

Yes, me. The dawning of recognition came when I was researching something for my blog, and I stumbled across an online site called Recovering Grace. It was a site created for young people who had been raised in the cult of ATI and now were finally telling their stories, as the cult leader, Bill Gothard, was being brought up on charges of improper behaviour toward young ladies. Within a few days I read the whole site, and there was more being added every day as young adults were coming forward with their stories. There was a spinoff group for parents like me. It's on Facebook and is called ATI Parent Recovery Group. I joined and started communicating for the first time with people all over North America who had lived the same reality as me. We compared stories about our children, our marriages, our churches and talked about how we dressed, how we homeschooled with no textbooks and how we felt. Most of it was talking about the damage that was done to us and our children under patriarchy.

And then I started talking. I never stopped. People were interested in what I had to say. They wanted to know all about my life.

They said, "You should write all this down."

I became obsessed with my past life. I finally realized that my first marriage had not been normal, and that I was still suffering trauma from that fundamentalist life many years after I'd been out. With my obsession there came the desire to write about it. It is powerful to write your story even if it is never published. In writing my story, I took back my life. I took it back from my past, from others who have judged and tried to define me, from a religious culture that had told me who I had to be, and even from my own limiting beliefs about myself.

But who would read it? What would be my reason for writing it? Aren't there lots of books out there about fundamentalist cults? Well, yes, there are, but they're all about young people who were raised in a cult. To my knowledge there are none about a wife and mother who raised her children in a cult, submitted to her husband in all things, and wore long dresses everywhere, even riding a bike, for fourteen years. There is nothing out there that I know of about how a wife and mother feels when she lays her career aside to homeschool her children according to the bible, and about how she felt during the years she was in a cult. Also about how she felt when she got out, how she reacted and how she started living her life again. But I didn't know if I should write my story because I didn't want to expose my ex or hurt my children. We'd been through enough.

This idea was never going to leave me. Several years after the fudge story, once again I found myself sitting around the table after a potluck supper when someone said, "Christine, you used to be in a cult didn't you?" I started talking and the more I talked, the more questions they asked.

"Tell us about how you dressed."

"Did you really do everything your husband wanted?"

"How could you possibly have taught your children from the bible?"

"Did your children go to university?"

"Didn't you feel that you were missing out on life? Did you not have a mind of your own?

"Why did you want to homeschool your children?"

And on it went.

A few years later, I was at a writer's conference, I was talking once again about my past and it became clear to me that the story was not about my ex or my children. It was about me and how I overcame the cult mentality of living under Patriarchy, submission and rules and regulations, and became a better, more sincere and compassionate woman than I would otherwise have been.

3

Meeting the Guy: Meant to Be?

At 28 years old, I felt like an old maid. Still single when most of my high school friends were married, all I needed was a cat to make my bachelor uncle's prediction come true. Uncle Jack never missed an opportunity to say, "The boys don't like fat girls. You'll be an old maid with a cat, maybe two, if you don't lose some weight." The reality was that I was only about ten pounds overweight, but that didn't stop Uncle Jack from criticizing me, at every opportunity. My self-confidence was in the gutter because of this, and I really believed that to find a man I had to be thin and beautiful.

It was 1982, I was 29 years old, and I was ready for something different. I had been teaching elementary school in Calgary for the previous eight years and I was getting restless. On a trip home to Newfoundland that summer, I wondered where my life was going. Mom was telling me about another two high school friends who had recently married, and others who were starting their families. I felt that something had to change in my life. I decided I would teach one more year at St Rose School in Calgary, and then it would be time to make a decision. It wasn't as if I had a lot of options at that point.

There were two: Option one would be to buy a condo in Calgary, furnish it and get some good china and crystal like my mother had, and then continue teaching until retirement. To this day, I'm not sure why I thought that route would bring me happiness. But I thought that's just what people do when they get older. Option two would be to quit teaching and go back to university and get a degree in counseling. I had always wanted to be a counselor because I loved helping people and I loved listening to them talk about their issues and problems. And I was getting tired of teaching little children. I should have been having my own little children.

Most of my friends were married and starting families at that point, and I was still the single teacher. I often wondered why I had been passed over. Maybe it was those ten pounds that Uncle Jack mentioned each summer I went home.

After spending a lovely two weeks with my family in Newfoundland in the summer of 1982, I ended up feeling quite fretful about my future. I was discussing this with my mom and my sister as we drove to the airport in Stephenville. We arrived at the airport where I would fly back to Calgary, via Montreal.

At the Eastern Provincial Airlines desk, the hostess frowned. "Oh, I'm so sorry, miss, but your plane left about an hour and a half ago."

"Well, shit."

I looked at my ticket in dismay.

"I think I read my arrival time in Montreal as my departure time from Stephenville. What can I do now?"

Thankfully that was back in the days when things were very casual and friendly between airlines. So, without too much fuss, I was put on another plane, an Air Canada jet, departing shortly, that would backtrack me to Gander where I would have to get off, line up for another boarding pass, and then fly directly from Gander to Montreal. And I wouldn't even miss the connection to Calgary!

Now why did that happen? Was Fate about to deal me something interesting?

Going through security in Stephenville, Newfoundland in 1982 meant passing through a glass door into a glass walled room, which served as the departure lounge. The people who were seeing you off were just on the other side of the glass. That would have been my mom and my sister. Sitting with his back to the glass wall but facing me was a man who was good looking in an outdoorsy sort of way. Out of the corner of my eye I could see him giving me the once over.

Well, at least I still have what it takes, I thought.

Behind him on the other side of the glass, my mother pointed to him as she mouthed the words, "He's cute. Sit with him on the plane."

I smiled.

The man thought I was smiling at him, but it was for my mom, right behind him.

It was not meant to be at that time because our seats had already been assigned. The man sat in the front of the plane, and I headed for my seat in the smoking section at the back. When we got off the plane in Gander and had to line up for new boarding passes, the stranger got in front of me in the line, turned and said, "Would you like to sit in non-smoking this time?"

"Sure, why not."

I can live without my cigarettes for a couple of hours. Besides, he's good looking, and that French accent is so sexy, I thought.

I took the window and the cute stranger sat in the aisle seat. We talked about many things on the four-hour flight from Gander to Montreal. He was starting his third year at Chiropractic College in Toronto and was headed to Trois Rivieres to see his family for a couple of weeks before returning to his studies. I told him about my teaching job in Calgary but that what I really wanted was to be married with children. I wanted to stay home to raise them, in a house with the proverbial white fence and a four-door car in the driveway. I wanted to decorate the house, cook, clean, and do all the things I had seen my mother do.

He said that he felt the same. He wanted to finish his Chiropractic studies and then have all the things I had spoken about. We were both amazed that we saw life in the same way. At that point, my inner dialogue was going crazy.

Good Lord, why am I telling all this to a perfect stranger? I will never see this man again, so it doesn't really matter what I say to him. We are just two people who met on a plane. He will return to his studies, and I will return to my two options.

"Do you believe in God?" he abruptly asked.

Well, since I wasn't an atheist and since I didn't follow Buddhism, Islam, or Mormonism, I said, "Of course." I had been raised Catholic but hadn't been inside the church in a long time. In fact, the last time I attended was so that the parish priest could see me there in order to give a recommendation for my teaching job in a Catholic school some years earlier.

This guy had just become 'born again', whatever that meant. He talked about giving his life to Jesus, but I had no idea what that meant either. There was a penetrating and intense look in his eyes as he told me that he had a personal relationship with Jesus. He seemed kind of strange with all his born-again jargon, but I didn't worry about that because I figured I would probably never see him again anyway. As the plane started its descent to Montreal, he turned to me.

"Would you write your address and phone number on this paper for me?

"Ok, and you can write yours down for me as well."

"No, I won't do that", he said, "because people exchange addresses all the time and then lose the paper, or never do get in touch. I'm taking your coordinates because I plan to contact you, very soon."

What the hell? Maybe this guy is a nut case after all. You never know who you might meet on a plane. He could be an axe murderer for all I know, and now he has my address and phone number. I should have given him the number for Calgary Pest Control instead.

And then we were on the ground, rushing through Arrivals, where his friend Etienne met him. There wasn't much time left to chat before I had to catch my next flight to Calgary, but there was just enough time for this guy to lean over and kiss me full on the lips.

Still swooning, I boarded my next flight bound for Calgary and sat there, fingers on my burning lips, wondering whether I would ever hear more from this mysterious, French, born again stranger.

4
Marriage and a Suitcase

I absolutely did hear from that Christian French guy again. In fact, he eventually became my husband in 1983, but not before he taught me all about being born again, witnessing, being saved and all that Christian terminology that I didn't understand on our first plane ride together.

He started writing and phoning me. I was an elementary school teacher in Calgary, and he was a Chiropractic student in Toronto, but he literally swept me off my feet. Sometimes I would find a rose tied on my apartment door when I went out in the morning. He had a contact in Calgary who did this for him. We had a phone code so that we each would know when one was thinking of the other. I would call his place in Toronto, let the phone ring once and hang up. If he was there and heard it, he would call me back and just let my phone ring once. That was back in the day when long distance phone calls were cost prohibitive.

I felt like I had the biggest secret in the world! Still teaching at a Catholic school in Calgary, I couldn't share my newfound love interest with any of them. How could I tell my Catholic counterparts that I was getting involved with a man who was not yet divorced from his estranged wife and who was a born-again Christian, not a Catholic. So, I didn't.

But in the middle of that school year, I resigned my teaching post in Calgary and moved to Toronto to be with him. Everyone thought I was pregnant, and the gossip was rampant.

Of course, I didn't know that at the time. Not until an acquaintance from Calgary came to visit me in Toronto for an overnight.

As we drove from the airport she said, "So Chris, you're not pregnant after all."

I'm sure I detected a note of disappointment in her voice. After spending some time together, I drove her back to the airport and never heard from her again.

Once my man had finished his Chiropractic studies in Toronto, we moved to Trois Rivieres, he to live with his parents and me to live in a third floor walk up apartment. On a memorable trip to Newfoundland to spend time with my parents, he finally proposed, after a 'chat' with my mother. My father had a jewelry store in Corner Brook, and he opened it one evening just for us to pick out a ring. It was fun to be the only ones in the store, with all the diamond rings out on the counter as I tried each one on. We chose one and then decided to get married that fall.

My parents were so excited to see their oldest daughter finally was going to get married. They took us for a ride in the car and we stopped at all their friends' places so they could make the wonderful announcement. At each house we were all invited in for a drink so they could meet and size up this person who was worthy of me. They were all quite happy and excited for my parents. Only in small town Newfoundland.

Finding a 'modest' wedding dress was going to be a problem. Modest in his Christian terms meant that it had to cover just about all my anatomy. I did find a beautiful dress, but the neckline was a little too low. Immodest! I bought it anyway and then had to try and find some lace to cover up the offending cleavage. Finally, my future sister-in-law gave me some lace from her wedding dress that worked perfectly. I sewed it onto my dress, and no one would ever have known it wasn't made like that.

We had a lovely wedding in the Catholic church where I had been baptized, received my first communion, first confession and confirmation, so you could see I was quite familiar with The Holy Redeemer Catholic church in Corner Brook, Newfoundland, nestled between Presentation high school for girls and Regina high school for boys. It was like coming home. All my parents' friends were there and some of mine. My old university friend Jenny came, but at the reception at my parents' house, she looked like she'd been crying. We had been best friends for years and it would be another 27 years before I found out why she looked like that on my wedding day.

Our honeymoon was in Puerto Vallarta, at a little resort. It was just beautiful. We behaved as newlyweds do, sharing our time between the beach and the hotel room. All was well.

We arrived home to Trois Rivieres to some nasty winter weather and with our suitcases in hand, we climbed the four flights of stairs to our apartment. As we arrived in our sparsely decorated new home, my husband set his suitcase on the living room floor and said, "Now that you are my wife, your body is not your own. It is mine and you have to submit." as per 1 Corinthians 4:7. And so began my 21-year marriage that ended when he left me for another woman. (And I breathed a sigh of relief). Such is the twisting of the scripture that can and did happen.

5

Getting into the Program

During the time my husband was a student at Chiropractic College in Toronto, he had read a book called The Late Great Planet Earth, by Hal Lindsey. I was to hear a lot about that book, which was one of the reasons he got himself saved in the first place. I eventually read it as well and learned about the doom and destruction that would come on all the non-Christians. There would be floods, famines, pestilences, and all sorts of horrors coming on the dammed (unsaved) So why wouldn't I get saved?

I didn't realize at the time there would always be famines, pestilences, and floods. Consider the flooding with global warming, and the Covid-19 pandemic of 2020 that lasted more than two years. Are they not the same thing? But I hadn't thought of that yet. It was a whole new world, so very foreign to me. I had been raised Catholic, and we never used those words. He told me about a seminar he had attended that had changed his life and he wanted me to learn what he had learned. And so, within a short period of time I was seated with him in a large forum at a weeklong Basic Seminar in Toronto, Ontario. It was given by a little man in a blue suit named Bill Gothard. Although in the years to come I never met the man in person, his name, his beliefs, and his teachings became a part of the fabric of our lives. It seemed to me at the time that this seminar was a prerequisite for us being a couple. It was also my introduction to the Institute in Basic Life Principles. The Seminar was long-- Monday to Thursday evenings and all-day Friday and Saturday.

The week flew as Bill told stories to illustrate his principles, all supported by scripture from the bible, and as he taught, I was captivated. Interestingly, in later years when I looked up those scriptures he had used to illustrate his points and principles, I didn't think they matched up. But who would question the little man in the blue suit? During that long week I learned a lot about God, the bible, and a Christian way of life. I learned that there were seven basic non-optional principles to live by that were the foundation of this Basic Seminar. Here they are:

Design: accepting the way God has made you, meaning your gender, your place in history, parents, siblings and where you were born. That's just a fancy way of saying self-acceptance.

Authority: respecting authorities (family, church, government, and employers) and staying under their "umbrella of protection". The umbrella of protection in families meant that God is head of the husband, and the husband is the head of the family, protecting them via an 'umbrella' of protection from Satan's fiery darts that could rain down on them. If the father had unconfessed sin in his life, it was symbolically seen as holes in the umbrella of protection on the wife and children. These holes would expose the family to Satan and all the evils of the world.

Responsibility: gaining and keeping a clear conscience. This meant that we are responsible to God for every thought, word, action, and motive. It also involved asking forgiveness from anyone we have offended so that no one could point a finger and say, "You've offended me and never asked for my forgiveness." I found myself phoning people that I hadn't seen or spoken to in several years and going over my 'crimes' and asking for forgiveness. For the most part, they thought I was nuts.

Suffering: learning to respond with forgiveness to those who offend us. This one was huge. Some people don't deserve our forgiveness, but we had to forgive them anyway. It's a given that people will offend us at some point, but we were to "…rejoice and be exceedingly glad" when people speak evil of us or persecute us.

Ownership: giving everything we own to God and yielding our rights to Him. In fact, we were taught that we had no rights and that we didn't own anything. It was all on loan from God. We could never take credit for all the hard work and study we endured to achieve our successes. We could never bask in the praise of our parents, teachers or friends because we were supposed to give all the glory to God or someone else. For example, if someone praised my son's excellent piano playing at a concert, he was supposed to say, "I had a great teacher, and that's why I did so well." Never mind all the hours and days of practice he did, he wasn't supposed to take credit.

Freedom: gaining moral purity through spiritual disciplines like bible reading, daily prayer and accountability. Moral freedom didn't mean that we could do what we wanted, but it was freedom to do what we should do based on Scripture. It's the idea of believing that the bible teachings are for our own good and for spiritual prosperity.

Success: discovering God's purpose for our lives and gaining spiritual power through meditation on Scripture. It also meant memorizing whole chapters of the bible, because God promises success for anyone who meditates on his word day and night. "For then you will make your way prosperous, and you will have good success." Joshua 1:8

I came away from that seminar crying and feeling like the most wretched sinner. It was a turning point in my life, the beginning of understanding something different about how to live. How could God have anything to do with me? There were also the distant rumblings of my feeling that I could never measure up to what was expected of me, by God or my husband. I would end up feeling like a failure on all fronts, in my own and everyone else's eyes. Of course, I learned that we are all sinners, saved by grace. It was at that point I became a born-again Christian and gave my life to the Lord. It meant that I was no longer a Catholic, but an Evangelical, attending a Pentecostal church. I was learning what exactly that meant and its cost. I started reading the bible and learning more and more about this new-to-me religion.

On a trip home to Newfoundland, my mother was dismayed to see my burgundy, leather-bound bible sitting on the bedside table. I'll never forget her incredulous expression when I told her that I was actually reading it. Most Catholics I knew didn't read the bible; that was for the priest. We had a huge family bible that sat on the coffee table and housed the family genealogy, but that was it.

Before long, we married, in 1983. For the first couple of years, we were pretty much like most people, and I maintained a good relationship with my family. It wouldn't always be like that. Soon enough, we heard that Bill Gothard had developed another seminar that took the basic principles to another level. The Basic Seminar was the prerequisite to attending the Advanced Seminar. It was also held in Toronto, and I went, this time with a nursing baby in tow. It was another weeklong seminar where we learned some new principles. These principles got more into the 'meat and potatoes' of the Christian life, taking verses from the bible literally and often out of context.

Here we learned to 'owe to no man, nothing at all', which meant there was to be no borrowing of money, not even for a house or a car. A Financial Freedom seminar was the spinoff of the Advanced Seminar, and we lapped it all up, even to the point of hosting a seminar at our church in Montreal. We paid off all our debts and started saving for a house which we eventually bought, paying cash for it. We saved up for our vehicles and when there was enough money, only then did we buy another car. It was a novel concept in a world where people borrow to improve their credit rating, and I have to say that we never experienced the stress that comes with large purchases, and we never had to pay thousands of dollars in interest.

We also learned that our family home should be a center of health, nutrition, and education. I became a voracious reader and educated myself on natural health and healthy eating. We learned the principles behind a successful marriage, how the wife was to 'reverence' her husband, and in turn the husband would 'love his wife as Christ loved the church'.

We were taught about home education as opposed to home 'schooling'. Homeschooling is just school at home whereas home education was teaching our children everything we knew from keeping a house, meal prep, changing the oil in the car, and getting the piano tuned. We were to home educate our children, protect them from the evil of the world and raise up a mighty generation to serve the Lord.

My husband was enchanted with the idea of home educating our children. I was not. Since we only had an infant at the time, I thought he would have a few years to get rid of that idea.

I was wrong. By the time our first son was six years old and the second one was four, we applied to be in the Advanced Training Institute of America This was Bill Gothard's home education program, all based at Headquarters in Oak Brook, Illinois. There was a long and involved application process that included many personal questions and many conditions. Some of them were:

-The men could not have beards or any other facial hair. We had to agree to this and send a photo of the family.
- The women were not allowed to wear pants, ever.
-Everyone in the family had to be enrolled in the program, even older children.
-We had to get all the music out of our home except for marches, classical music and hymns. No Christian rock. No TV.
-We needed a couple of letters of reference.

I could feel my life slipping away as we filled out the form. No pants for me, ever? What about riding my bike? Hiking? Little did I realize that once we were in, I would not put on a pair of pants, sweats or shorts for the next fourteen years.

I kept thinking they would never accept us; we just weren't that kind of people, but about six weeks after we sent in the application an acceptance letter arrived in the mail. I didn't know whether to be happy or dismayed. We knew a couple of families who had applied and were rejected. They were given a list of things to do in order to apply the following year. So much was the pull of ATI they did every item and were accepted.

After our acceptance, we had to go to Knoxville Tennessee for yet another week-long seminar to become indoctrinated and to get our learning materials. In 1991 there were no programs for the younger children, so my parents-in-law came to our place to take care of them. I had a sense of fearful anticipation as to how our lives were about to change drastically.

6
What is it About Suitcases?

The night before we left for Knoxville for what would be the first of many ATI seminars, I had a meltdown as I stared into my empty suitcase. I had packed my underwear, one dress and a notebook. That was it. Women attending the Advanced Training Institute of America conference were told they were not to wear pants. Only dresses and skirts would be suitable. Far below the knee dresses and skirts. It made me cry when I looked at all the beautiful clothing in my closet but would not be able to bring to the conference. We were leaving the next day for the two-day drive to Knoxville Tennessee where we would be indoctrinated for a whole week on Biblical Principles and a new way of life.

We were going to be an ATI homeschooling family. My husband and I had read and signed the papers with all the rules and regulations of being in this exciting phase of our lives. It was just that it didn't feel very exciting. It felt more like a prison. We weren't allowed to have a TV in the house, all family members were to be enrolled in the program, and there were to be no textbooks; only the Bible and the 54 Wisdom Booklets that would be provided. The curriculum was all based on the Sermon on the Mount, a verse or two per month. We had completed the four-page application form, written the letters affirming our faith, papers were sent to 'Headquarters' affirming that neither of us had a criminal record, and my husband had shaved his moustache. He had to do that because there was no facial hair to be allowed on any ATI father.

I only had two dresses, the ones I wore on alternate Sundays for church. But now they were telling me that I had to wear skirts and dresses for the weeklong conference and thereafter as a homeschooling mom. That's why the suitcase was empty--there was nothing to put in it.

As I sobbed, cried and lamented our choice to enroll in such a strict organization, my husband sat beside me on the bed, feeling helpless. I don't think he could begin to understand what I was giving up. Honestly, since this was more his idea than mine, I was sure at that point that he would have promised me anything to just get me there and get started.

"It's easy enough for you", I wailed, "All you have to do is pack pants and tops and away you go. Why are they doing this to the women?"

"Because women should be dressed like women, not like men, and besides, it's more modest. When you wear a skirt, no man can see the outline of your body. That's meant only for me."

"I hate this program already."

And with that, he promised me we would leave a few days early so that I could buy the much-needed skirts and dresses. We couldn't have me shaming my husband by being dressed inappropriately. We would go to the outlets in Pigeon Forge, Tennessee. It was about an hour from Knoxville and would be a nice time of shopping and sightseeing.

With that promise in mind, I closed my empty suitcase and my husband put it in the car before I could change my mind.

"Hopefully it will be full when we come back."

With my parents-in-law taking care of the children during our time away, there was nothing to worry about on that front. We had a wonderful relationship with them, and they loved their grandsons. It was a special time for all of them.

And so, we left Montreal and drove to Pigeon Forge, Tennessee for some serious shopping. There were a couple of major outlets, Tanger and Belz, and we went in every ladies shop they had. Eddie Bauer, Anne Klein, Dress Barn, Columbia and Anne Taylor, no shop was left unsearched. And at the end of two days shopping, I spread out my haul on the hotel room bed. I had enough clothing to last for a long time. There were dresses, skirts, sweaters, and baggy tee shirts, all so that I could be presentable and feminine for this new way of life.

Buying all those clothes didn't make me feel any more feminine or comfortable though. I always had thought that clothing was a form of self-expression, but these clothes were just not me. I had always been a jeans and T shirt kind of woman and liked funky clothing and cowboy boots. I wondered what my family would think of the new modest me. But the worst was that now I had to wear all the things I had bought. What would I do with all the shorts and jeans I had at home? And what about a bathing suit? Surely if pants were immodest, then bathing suits had to be completely scandalous.

After our shopping spree, we made our way to the University of Tennessee campus where we had booked a dorm room. It was a beautiful campus, filled with blooming magnolia trees and shaded pathways. Every day we walked from the dorm to the auditorium for the lectures, and then to the cafeteria for meals. There would be no toast and peanut butter for breakfast, just something called hush puppies and grits. This southern food was quite different for us people from the north. Back and forth we went for breakfast, lunch and dinner. It was so hot that July in the south, we were both sweating on the walks to and fro and freezing in the air-conditioned auditorium.

And the auditorium-- the first evening we went to the Thompson Boling Arena for the lectures, given by Bill Gothard himself, I could see the magnitude of what we were getting ourselves into. Huge banners that hung from the rafters proclaimed, "Giving the World a 'New' way of Life." The auditorium was packed; there were well over ten thousand people just like us, searching for success in life. There seemed to be a lot of pregnant women; either that or they were overweight. It was hard to tell because most of the women were wearing loose jumpers or dresses. And it seemed that they all had long hair, down past their shoulders with half of it pulled back with a bow that matched their dresses. When I asked one woman when her baby was due and she told me she wasn't pregnant, I learned to keep my mouth shut.

Looking around, I saw that with my new clothes I did fit in. I'm not saying that it felt good or bad, it just was. I looked pretty much like all the other ATI moms, except my hair wasn't long enough yet and I hadn't learned to say, "Y'all".

I realized that we were just getting into the homeschooling movement. People had been homeschooling, especially in the United States for awhile already. At the seminar we learned that homeschooling was illegal in some states, like Texas, and fathers were being arrested because their children were truant.

We got home from that seminar with a car full of books, a new curriculum, and high hopes. For the next fourteen years I home educated my children without textbooks, just that dammed curriculum. They learned to read from bible passages, and the curriculum changed every four weeks. We were becoming more and more peculiar every day. I had no idea at this point that we were in a cult. That realization of truth would come many years later.

Every four weeks of those homeschooling years, I cried. I cried out of frustration with the ATI program. I cried because I couldn't measure up. I cried because all my friends were out having coffee and shopping and I was home in a long dress, homeschooling my children and feeling inadequate most of the time. I had become one of those holy rollers that I used to ridicule. It might have seemed strange in other circumstances that I, Christine Faour, who had recited 'The Night of the King's Castration' from the top of a snowbank many years prior, was now talking Christian jargon in a modest, long dress while trying to reverence her husband and home educate her sons to become godly young men.

7
Homeschooling in ATI

After that first Knoxville seminar we had a new outlook on life, four hundred dollars' worth of new books, my new clothes, our new curriculum and a new sewing machine. Everything was new. It was almost like a rebirth. Since whole families were enrolled, and not individuals, my husband and I were to learn along with our children. I was dubious about being successful with this program because we were to teach our children through a series of 'Wisdom Booklets' instead of textbooks. There were 54 of them. These Wisdom Booklets were the foundation of the Advanced Training Institute's education plan. They were based on the Sermon on the Mount (Matthew 5-7). Each booklet used one or two verses to teach language, math, medicine, law and history. With illustrations, graphs and pictures we were taught how God's word permeates every aspect of our lives. The presentation was excellent though, and very convincing. We were to complete one booklet each month and eight of them over the course of a school year. It took between seven and eight years to complete them all. Then we were to start over and do them again, the assumption being that the children would be older and get more out of them at that time.

That was pretty hard for this former teacher to swallow. I had been used to following curriculum guides and their accompanying textbooks. Just to show how the booklets were designed, the Sermon on the Mount starts with,

"And seeing the multitudes, he went up into a mountain."

From this one verse we learned about eyesight and eye problems, how many people made a multitude, what are the great mountains of the world and how to see the world around us. One of the projects from that first wisdom booklet had us all dressed up and sitting on a bench in the mall to observe what the other people were wearing and how they related to each other. We were very judgmental of just about everyone because of how they were dressed, if their hair was unruly, whether or not they had tattoos, and whether the children were obedient to their parents. Then we went home to discuss it and we prided ourselves on the fact that we weren't like those people.

Since we believed every word and felt that we were doing God's will we figured that it would all be ok. I actually did teach my oldest son to read using the bible. I had been a schoolteacher for the ten years prior to enrolling in ATI and I was as brainwashed as the rest of the "Gothardites" as we were sometimes called. Everything I knew to be true from my days of teaching in schools went out the window as I embraced this 'new way of life'.

Every four weeks as we finished a wisdom booklet, we had to send in a report to 'Headquarters'. This was a big building in Oak Brook, Illinois that was the heart of the organization. Every four weeks as my husband and I tried to fill out these impossible reports on our children who were four and six in the first year, my brain started to fry. Literally, it felt as if something was happening to my brain such that I couldn't focus on those darn reports. So I just filled in any old thing because I didn't think anyone was ever going to look at them anyway. To this day I don't believe anyone did look at them. And I cried. I cried every four weeks because that was about the length of time I was able to hold it together before breaking down.

Speaking of breaking down, I felt that I was having a nervous breakdown throughout the time we were in ATI, but I didn't have time to give in to it. I was too busy pasting on the smile, wearing my long floral dresses and trying to be supermom while giving my children an outstanding school experience and catering to my husband.

People who came to our house during the cult years were amazed at the tidy home, the obedient and helpful children and the perfection that permeated everything. They had no idea of what went on in the hour before they arrived at our 'perfect' home. The scurrying around to clean up, tidy up and make things presentable put an incredible pressure on all of us. I remember trying to make the place look perfect, going so far as to putting a polished, silver flute on the immaculate coffee table with a silk rose beside it.

While I was trying to do all this, most moms with young children were just trying to survive and get through the day.

Some of them used to say to me, "I could never do all that you're doing."

My usual response was, "I can't do it either."

But they never believed me. Little did they know that I was constantly on the brink of having a nervous breakdown. The pressure to perform was incredible. That's what happens when you're not true to yourself and your life is fit into a mold of someone else's' making. I felt like such a fake and wondered what these people would think if they knew what I was really like, on the inside. There were so many demands put on me that I often wished I could go somewhere to have that nervous breakdown. But there was never time.

  One of our Wisdom Booklets talked about the grain of wheat in the bible, and about how Jesus could have compared himself to just about anything or anyone, but he compared himself to bread. He called himself the Bread of Life. In calling Himself the Bread of Life, He is saying that ultimately, he can satisfy our deepest needs and longings. He can make us feel 'full' and overflowing with blessing. I never experienced that, but the analogy was interesting.

  On the practical side, we also learned all about wheat and how grinding it ourselves to make bread would keep all the nutrition and fiber that's supposed to be in it. With that in mind, we bought a grain mill and got in contact with someone who could regularly sell us 44 lb bags of organic wheat from Saskatchewan. I started making bread, and at the outset I can tell you I made every mistake that was possible. And I learned. I learned about what makes the bread rise, how to develop the gluten in the dough, how to add things to make it even healthier and what vitamin C, or ascorbic acid could do to help the consistency of the finished product. I learned so much that I began to teach others how to make bread from scratch and soon enough I became known as the Bread Lady. My boys also learned how to make it and sold the loaves in the downstairs clinic for $3 per loaf. The bread was delicious. At first, I spent so much time making it that sometimes our meal would consist of bread and nothing else. And I wondered why I constantly had IBS. I never made the connection until many years later. I had a sensitivity to wheat, or the gluten in it.

I still have my grain mill and all the bread making paraphernalia. Sometimes even now, I make a few loaves and it is just as delicious as back in those days, or so my present husband tells me. I still grind the wheat berries in my Whisper Mill so that the resulting flour has all the bran, but more importantly, the wheat germ, which is still living. The flours and breads we buy today have the wheat germ taken out because of the spoiling factor. I've included the recipe in the Appendix at the end of this book.

8

Weird, Peculiar or Just Plain Stupid?

We were so different that we never taught the children about Santa Claus. They knew that the Christmas gifts came from Mom and Dad and that other children believed in a fat man in a red suit that came down the chimney with his bag of gifts and then he disappeared back up the chimney where his sleigh and reindeer were waiting for him on the roof. Other children would tell what Santa had brought them but ours said their gifts came from their parents. We believed in the significance of the fact that the letters in the word Santa could be rearranged to spell Satan.

Now, don't get me started on Halloween. We believed that Halloween came straight from the pit of hell with all the talk of ghouls, goblins, ghosts, witches, and skeletons. The costumes were downright frightening. We just couldn't understand why other people celebrated this feast of the dead. And when the churches had an alternative Halloween activity, with the children dressing up as biblical characters, we stayed away from that as well. I remember telling the organizers that replacing Halloween with a biblical activity was still celebrating Halloween. So, on October 31 every year we turned off all the lights upstairs and watched a movie in the basement. Or we went out to eat. One year we were at McDonalds having a quiet burger and fries when someone walked past our table dressed like Freddy Krueger. It was horrifying for my sheltered children. That was the end of eating out on Halloween. There was no way we were going to expose our children to those evils. The next day when all the candy was half price I'd go to Walmart and buy some for my boys because I didn't want them to miss out.

There were times when glimpses of my childhood in Newfoundland came to mind. I thought of the costumes my friends and I wore, sometimes over a snowsuit because there were years when winter came early, and we had to climb over snowbanks to cross the street. But we loved every moment.

And I thought of going to bed on Christmas Eve when I was young. The house would be quite normal when my brother and I went to bed, but we knew that something magical would happen overnight. We'd creep down the stairs in the wee hours and the house would have been transformed. There was always a huge tree, all lit up and glowing in the darkness, and the gifts were on display underneath. Peeking out from behind the tree was a life size poster of Santa Claus drinking a bottle of coca cola. It was magnificent! My children never got to experience anything like that. The mystery and wonder of childhood were lost on them. It made me sad to think that they would never have what I had when I was young. During that time, I often asked myself if I had had an evil childhood. At the time I wasn't sure but today I know that my childhood was wonderful, magical, protected and innocent. I wouldn't trade it for anything

As we enrolled in ATI, we had to get rid of the TV because of all the perceived evil emanating from it. We had a nice TV and didn't want to throw it out so we put it in a closet, and it came out every fall so my husband could watch football games that his friend had taped for him. We were not connected to any kind of cable service. We had been taught about the evils of TV. We learned that there were unsavory sorts of people, crooks, criminals, murderers and the like that we would never open our doors to, but when you turn on a TV, you're inviting them into your house. It made sense to me at the time.

Then there was the food. At one point we learned about the Levitical laws concerning meats. In Leviticus 17:13-14 it states that the life of any creature is in the blood. Therefore, we were not to consume the blood of any animal. (Blood pudding lovers beware). But the taste of most meats is in the blood, or as we often call it, the juices. Here we were, not supposed to eat an animal's blood. I'll never forget the time we were invited to a close friend's place for a lovely steak supper. They had bought expensive cuts of meat for us, the honored guests. My husband took our steaks and rinsed them under tap water until the water ran clear and the meat was a garish shade of grey. Our hosts cooked them anyway on the BBQ and truthfully, they tasted awful. We were never invited back.

You might be wondering, with the emphasis on modesty for the females, how we would ever be able to go for a swim. I couldn't possibly wear a normal bathing suit, could I? What about wearing shorts and a t-shirt for swimming? How about not swimming at all? As ATI and the homeschooling movement grew, so did several home businesses that catered to the different lifestyle. One was called Lilies Apparel. I found them online and bought a couple of modest dresses from them. They also had a bathing suit model if you could call it a bathing suit. It sure did cover what modest ATI females wanted covered. I ordered one in a black and floral print. I thought I wouldn't wear a two-piece bathing suit again in my life, but I never considered wearing a three-piece one. First there was the pants which went just about to my knees. Then there was a camisole type of top, and lastly, the dress that went over it all, which was baggy and effectively hid any feminine shape. It also had frills around the shoulders for an alluring and feminine effect.

I remember proudly wearing my modest bathing suit while visiting my parents in Florida. My mother said not one word until years later, but I had embarrassed her and Dad. It's incredible what a little brainwashing can do to your wardrobe.

There were so many ways that we made ourselves different from others that we stood out, and not in a good way. We had an answer to every objection to our way of life. We were taught how to answer to our critics, and we learned it well, so well in fact, that we believed it ourselves. Why else would we have continued in this peculiar life? Or was it weird, or just plain stupid?

Our children were indoctrinated along with us. In fact, one of my son's writing assignments was to write about all the ways we were different from most people. That wasn't too difficult; in his list were things like, Mommy wears dresses, we homeschool, we make all our food from scratch, among others. We were foolishly proud of our differences.

9

One Day I Woke Up Happy

During the fourteen years we homeschooled in the cult of ATI, I woke up every morning with a sense of dread and a pain in my gut. I felt unworthy for this lofty role of being a Christian homeschooling mom. I didn't feel spiritual at all. And even though I had been a schoolteacher for many years, this was something entirely new. Teaching children with no other textbook than the bible was nothing that university had prepared me for. I managed, but felt that somehow, someone was going to find out that our children were homeschooled with no books and either make us put them in school or take them away from us. The fear was constantly with me, but I kept telling myself that we were doing the right thing for the children, even though I knew in my heart that it wasn't the right thing.

  I had been out to buy groceries one cold February day and when I came home there was a notice from the post office on the door. The books that I had been awaiting had finally arrived, but I wasn't home to receive them. I could get them at the postal outlet the next day. That night I slept with visions of new books dancing in my head. In the morning, I woke up with a smile on my face, got up, dressed, and readied myself to go out into the cold and snowy February day to get my books. On my way to the postal outlet in the nearby mall I felt an ominous clunking coming from the rear of the car and realized that I had a flat tire. I called my husband and he sent someone from the garage to fix the tire. That took the better part of an hour. I didn't care because when that was over, I was going to have my books.

When I got to the postal outlet, they told me that my package had been left at another postal outlet and that I could pick it up tomorrow. My hopes had gone up and down so many times I didn't know what to think at that point. But I was undaunted. Can you imagine a life so tedious that the mere anticipation of new books could change my disposition?

That afternoon my husband and I went to Tim Horton's for a coffee. As we sipped, he said, "I have a question for you."

Fearing the worst, because I never knew what might be coming, I asked him what the question was.

"This morning you woke up happy. You never wake up happy. Why was that?"

Ah, so he noticed. I told him the reason for my great joy was that I had books waiting for me at the post office and I couldn't wait to pick them up.

"Well," he said, "It doesn't take much to make you happy."

I remember telling him that I hated my life and felt pressured all the time to be someone I was not capable of being. I felt that I could never measure up. Never.

The truth was that I could not experience joy if I was living a life that was contrary to everything I believed and the way I was raised. I was not able to be true to myself because in the cult I was obliged to dress a certain way, act a certain way, live a certain way and even to speak in a specified manner. My children had to be perfect and neither I nor anyone else was ever able to make that happen. Children are not perfect, miniature adults. They are learning machines, messy, loud, fun, defiant, dirty, snotty, cuddly, transparent bundles of energy that are ready for anything.

My joy had been long ago squashed. My light had gone out with the oppression and demands made on my life by the ATI standards. I was not able to be spontaneous, not able to be myself. It has been many years since I lived that life and it's only recently that I have finally started to rediscover who I really am and to find my old self.

I know that 'finding myself' is an overused cliché of our times, but during those years I had really become lost as to who I was, where I came from, my roots, but most of all I had lost my 'joie de vivre'. My parents and siblings couldn't understand who I had become.

Joy of living? Joy of the Lord, and those other smiling things were not evident in my life. I hated my life, so it was kind of hard to feel joyful when I was dying inside.

Back then I don't think I had any idea what real joy was. But these days I'm starting to figure it out. That day at Tim Horton's I told my husband not only that I hated my life, but I felt so harried that I constantly thought I was headed for a nervous breakdown but that there was no time for it. I broke down crying right there at Tim Horton's and wailed about the life I was missing out on. But there was nothing to be done. We were in this life, and I thought there was no way out of it.

    The next day I did go to the other postal outlet and picked up my books. For just a few days I was able to escape into the world of my books and feel like a real person again.

10

Can I have a Nervous Breakdown Now?

Every morning we woke up to loud 'Godly' music from a little boom box, which was placed in the hallway so it could be heard from every bedroom. It blasted us all out of bed. Time to get perfectly dressed, right down to the shoes, tidy the bedrooms and then meet at 7 AM in the kitchen for a Wisdom Search. This consisted of reading a chapter from Proverbs and five Psalms every morning. We took turns reading aloud and then discussing what we learned from the readings. In Proverbs there is a lot of reference made to fools. So, we would discuss who was acting like a fool or being foolish. Sometimes it was one of my sons who was acting that way and he would be shamed into behaving himself. In reality, what we referred to as foolishness and fools was simply young boys being boys and having fun. When I think of it, there was not much fun in our lives, not much laughter and not a whole lot of joy. It was more like eating prunes and all bran every day of our lives. Constipated.

Most years, in June we went to Knoxville Tennessee for our homeschooling convention for more training, or you could say, more brainwashing. The men would have early morning sessions with the little guy (Bill Gothard) himself. And every morning they were told to guard their daughters from divorced men. There would be no divorce. But what about the men present who were already divorced and had remarried before 'getting into the program'? My husband fell into that category and with this message pounded into his head every morning, he felt more and more shamed and inadequate.

Do you know about the TV series, 19 Kids and Counting? It portrayed the Duggar family as they daily lived out their homeschooling roles, in their house. They are an ATI family, and all their children were enrolled in the program. They were what we called a 'poster family' because they were an example to the rest of us on how to lead a family, reverence the husband, dress modestly, juggle their time, and all the rest. They even gave conferences for ATI and I'm sure that everyone else wished they could be like the Duggars. There were other families that we looked up to as well.

There was another family where the father worked at 'Headquarters', and the whole family were musicians, in addition to following the ATI lifestyle. The pressure to measure up must have been incredible because eventually the father left to be with his secretary, while his wife and children were left holding the proverbial bag. It was shocking because we all thought that our marriages were super protected. We were told that if we followed the basic principles and did everything we were taught to do, we would have successful marriages and successful children. We've since found out the untruth of that. Things happen, people are human. Really, they are.

But back to the Knoxville training conferences. Once programs had been developed for them, our three sons came with us to Knoxville. Most years that was the family vacation, and it was fun for them. While the parents attended sessions, the boys were enrolled in a program called Alert Cadets. It was sort of like a boot camp for boys under 16 years old. They learned about character qualities, bible stories and the lives of some great Christians. And they marched in formation, just like an army for God.

The women had sessions where we were taught how to reverence our husbands, cook from scratch, and train our children 'in the way they should go'. Training the children meant, "Spare the rod and spoil the child", in other words, punishing them every time they did something wrong. Evidently, I wasn't doing it right. We had a visit from our family coordinators in the second year of homeschooling. Family coordinators were simply adolescents who were also in ATI. Ethan and Ryan were going around the country visiting ATI families to give encouragement and help. They taught us how to really spank the children, with a 'rod of correction'. At first, we used a wooden dowel to spank but they kept breaking and I ended up buying a wooden paddle from a craftsperson in the area. This was made to have been a wall decoration once it was tole painted. I didn't paint mine. This paddle was so thick it would never break. Sometimes I quietly cried to myself while spanking my boys. In my heart it just wasn't right. But this is what we were told to do, and it was reinforced when we went to the training seminars in Knoxville.

Babies were not exempt. We were shown how to 'blanket train' an infant. Thankfully, by the time I learned of this

I had no infants. I'm ashamed for having used the rod of correction rather than being patient and showing more love to my children. I've since asked their forgiveness for this and other things as well.

We were also taught that it was God who opened and closed the womb, so who were we to decide when and how many children to have? Every year there was a special time at the conference when all the moms with 'reversal babies' would parade across the stage with their babies. These were women who at some point had a sterilization procedure but, because of the teachings, decided to have a reversal surgery of their sterilization. If it was the husband who had a vasectomy, then he would get it reversed. There were a lot of reversal babies, many born to couples who had thought their families were finished years ago.

Honestly, some of the women I met down there in Tennessee every summer looked more and more haggard and worn out as the string of children behind them increased year after year. I guess I was one of the lucky ones because I married late and had my three children by the time I was 40, but I had also had two miscarriages. I mention the miscarriages because they happened one before and one during the homeschooling years. There was no such thing as taking time to heal my body and grieve my lost babies. I had to soldier on and keep smiling, keep cooking and keep homeschooling my sons as if nothing had happened.

When family members came to visit, they often remarked on how much I'd changed. They didn't know me anymore. I wasn't the same as I'd used to be. In place of my old self was a supermom who kept pushing through the obstacles and who made sure her children were perfect.

My children never knew the real Christine, their mom. Instead, I was their taskmaster and teacher, and it broke my heart. I tried so hard for us to be perfect, good examples to other families. Why couldn't we just be a normal family? I felt we never measured up because we had to follow all those standards. But we were reminded time and again of the verse that says, "Man looks on the outward appearance, but God looks at the heart." And yet, there was so much emphasis on how we looked, how we dressed, how our children dressed and behaved that the pressure was constant. I remember needing a nap every single afternoon just to get through the day and sometimes I said to no one in particular, "I think I'm having a nervous breakdown but there is no time and no one to acknowledge it to me." It was a horrible feeling, that sensation that I was always on the brink of a crash.

Outwardly, I was living the life of a Pharisee, proclaiming my own goodness and perfection, and trying to help others to do the same. But inside I felt broken and emotionally battered. I was the only one who knew I was pretending, and there I was, telling everyone that my life was wonderful and the people who came to me for advice believed every word I said. I was trapped in my good-wife and mother role and felt like a phony every time.

11

The Proverbs 31 Woman

When speaking of homeschooling in ATI and what it was like to be a homeschooling mom and submitted wife, there is no avoiding the Proverbs 31 woman. Out of all 1,189 chapters in the Bible, this is the one that made most of us women feel inadequate and ashamed of all we were not accomplishing. It didn't matter that we were having babies, making all our food from scratch, homeschooling our children, dressing like nuns and submitting to our husbands. Proverbs 31 was the gold standard for every ATI woman.

When I first read about it, I thought the Proverbs 31 woman was overwhelmingly perfect. I wanted to be like her. However, over time the scepter of this perfect woman was just something else to pound me over the head at all the things I was lacking in my efforts.

Who is the Proverbs 31 woman anyway? According to The World English Bible translation, here are some of her highlights:

Hymn to a Good Wife

Who can find a worthy woman?
For her price is far above rubies.
The heart of her husband trusts in her.
He shall have no lack of gain.

She does him good, and not harm,
all the days of her life.
She seeks wool and flax,
and works eagerly with her hands.
She is like the merchant ships.
She brings her bread from afar.
She rises also while it is yet night,
gives food to her household,
and portions for her servant girls.

She perceives that her merchandise is profitable.
Her lamp doesn't go out by night. She opens her arms to the poor;
yes, she extends her hands to the needy.
She makes for herself carpets of tapestry.
She makes linen garments and sells them,
Strength and dignity are her clothing.
She looks well to the ways of her household,
and doesn't eat the bread of idleness.
Her children rise up and call her blessed
Her husband also praises her;
Many women do noble things
but you excel them all."

Of course, we didn't read The WEB translation of the bible. We read the New king James Version, which we thought was more accurate but also more difficult to understand, another form of spiritual snobbery on our part. In summary, the Proverbs

31 woman makes her own clothing, she knits, she sews, she gets up before dawn to prepare for the day, she buys a field and gardens it, she helps the poor and she goes to work, all with a smile and words of kindness. Even her husband praises her.

Can you imagine trying to be all of that? Can you imagine the pressure? I tried hard to be a Proverbs 31 woman, but you know, it's not easy. Some days I made food from scratch, some days I did other things. I did crafts. I hosted dinner parties. I took care of my family. Every day I homeschooled my children, and every couple of weeks I cried. I cried because the stress of trying to fit into this mould and the shame of not being able to do it eventually wore me down. I don't know of a human being who has been able to be all of those things and not have a nervous breakdown or a marriage breakup. I was tired all the time. No wonder! I watched my non-homeschooling friends go for coffee together or shopping and wondered what had become of my life. I didn't have the energy to join them, and even if I did, I didn't have the time. I longed for a life that wasn't so complicated and demanding. I didn't feel that there was room for individuality; I was to be a clone of every other denim jumper-wearing ATI mom.

It's not that there's anything wrong with doing the things a proverbs 31 woman does. It's just that to tell someone they must do and be all that is stated therein is cruel. To even try to be like 'that' woman was enough to make the strongest of us depressed. And if that wasn't bad enough, on ATI mom's email support chain, someone mentioned a business called ScriptureWear. They said it was a place where you could buy brooches that depicted certain passages of scripture and were made by stay-at-home moms in North Carolina. Intrigued, I checked it out. Sure enough, there was a Proverbs 31 brooch, just what every fundamentalist homeschooling mom needs to sport on her denim jumper.

The brooch depicts some of the aspects of the Proverbs 31 woman: prayer, cooking, organized time, grapes from the garden, etc.

I have to tell you that I bought the brooch and actually wore it a couple of times on my denim jumper. And then I didn't. It was a conspicuously cumbersome brooch and invited questions as to what it meant and why I was wearing it. If I tried to explain that to someone not in the cult, they would have thought I was nuts. In hindsight, I think I was a bit off the wall myself. So, in 1999 I put the brooch in my jewelry box and to this day it is still there. Another ATI mom mentioned to me that the only thing missing from that brooch was a ball and chain. I concur. I don't know why I still have it; I've put it in the garbage a couple of times but always have gone back to retrieve it. Maybe I keep it as a reminder to just be myself and not worry about trying to fit into someone else's idea of who and what I should be ever again.

The brooch always reminded me that I wasn't good enough the way I was and that I never would be good enough. [1]

When my husband left me for another woman a few years later, the shame, depression and hardship I went through made the Proverbs 31 woman look like a farce to me. Believe me, I

---

[1] A photo of my Scripturewear brooch can be seen in the Appendix.

had tried hard to be the best wife I knew how to be, but in the end, it was all for naught. I thought that if I followed all the guidelines of what made a godly wife, that my marriage would be safe. Obviously, my plans didn't work; divorce happened, and depression came as I tried to pick up the broken dreams and pieces of my life.

12

Honey, have you Felt the Pain?

During the time my family lived in the confines of ATI, I felt that every aspect of our lives were ordered. We never had to worry about what to wear nor what was in fashion at the time because we were told how to dress and to draw attention to our countenances with scarves and short necklaces. God forbid that we would wear a V neck top or a long necklace; those things would draw the eye downward to our breasts. We didn't wear patterned stockings because men would be looking at our legs. No skirt slits and everything we wore had to be mid-calf, the most unflattering skirt length for anyone. I remember one young woman who had a long, straight skirt with a slit. She sewed up the slit but then had to walk like a geisha because there was so little room.

      We were warned about what toys would be dangerous to our children, in particular the Cabbage Patch Dolls. We were taught that they were demonic and that they had middle names of demons, like Gwenda, Mariusa, Atalie and Lester. Thankfully I didn't have daughters, so a decision never had to be made on that front. However, I do remember throwing out my son's Teenage Mutant Ninja Turtles because he liked them too much. What kind of a mom does something like that?

      In marriage, a man's role is to provide "servant leadership" while "the woman responds with reverent submission and assistance, taught Bill Gothard, who has never been married. He made himself an authority on marriage relationships. He even told us when the best time was to have sex in order to favor conception. We were to only have sex between days 15 and 28 of the wife's menstrual cycle. Days 8-14 are maybe okay, but if you're trying to be ultra-Godly, or get pregnant, wait until day 15. You want the "seed" as strong as possible. He taught us how to have a good relationship and how the wife was to 'reverence' her husband and in turn the husband would love the wife as Christ loved the church. Reverence my husband? Is reverence as a verb even a word? How are you supposed to do that? My understanding at the time was that I was to obey him, trust in him, gaze at him when he speaks and in general, to treat him with deference, reverence and respect. As one woman understood it, she was to treat her husband as if he were Christ and how she would treat him if he were living in her home.

We learned how to deal with depression: declutter the house and play Godly music. Seriously? What about all the women who had tidy homes and were still on depression medications?

We had almost succeeded in making our home a center of nutrition, education, financial freedom, health and hospitality, at a great cost to my personal freedom and my family's lightheartedness. It often felt as if our lives were lived according to a set of rules and regulations and there was no room for fun, creativity and spontaneity.

Believing everything I heard at the annual seminars in Knoxville Tennessee, I was pretty sure that my family and I were insulated from all the evils of the world and that fact made me feel quite smug about the outward and perceived success of my life. If I just followed all the guidelines and lists on how to live a successful and prosperous life and submitted to my husband, I would be spared. You can imagine my attitude when I went to a ladies retreat given by my church during that time. I went in feeling that I was better than just about everyone else present and that I had nothing left to learn. I think I was the only person in a modest dress: below the knees and up to the neck; the others were all in jeans or pants. I judged them for that. I couldn't see my prideful attitude at all.

I remember on the Saturday of the retreat; the leader was talking about 'the pain'. I listened, but truthfully, I had no idea what pain she was talking about. Pain? I didn't have any pain in my life; my children were doing great, I thought I had a good marriage, we were all healthy, no one in my extended family had died, so where was the pain? I had conveniently forgotten about my miscarriages and grieving my lost babies. I forgot how I so often cried out to God to make me a better wife. I forgot how sad I was because my parents rarely came to visit. I believe that my pain was stuffed so far down in my psyche that to pull it up would have cracked my smiling mask. I just wasn't able to admit my pain to myself or anyone else. In my mind that day, I had no pain.

The leader kept talking about the pain and how we were to give it up to Jesus. "Humble yourselves, admit your pain, give it up to Jesus and let it all out." Before long, she was crying as she told us about things that had happened in her life and her pain, and most of the other women were crying too as they recalled their pain. One mourned her father's death; another mourned the estrangement of her daughter; another had been raped when she was younger; some had been abandoned, others suffered from depression. I couldn't relate because nothing like that had ever happened to me. I kind of felt badly because I had nothing to cry about. I thought that if only all those women could follow the life principles that I was following, they would not have so much pain in their lives.

As the women got more emotional and let out their pain, we were instructed to get off our chairs and kneel in front of them, putting our faces on the seat. Now we could cry out to God about our pain. But I had no pain, not any that I was willing to admit, even to myself. I couldn't just sit there, could I? So, I did what the others did, putting my face on the chair just to not stick out, but I had no idea of the depth of their pain and suffering. With my face on the chair, I could hear the other women crying. I was stoic with my head on the chair. Some were wailing and calling out to God. And then, I dared to lift my head and peek at the other women. No one noticed me because they were so busy with their own unique misery. As I looked around the room of about thirty-five women all with their faces on their chairs, crying and praying, I couldn't believe my eyes. I was numb.

How could I have gotten to 45 years old and not felt 'the pain'? I racked my brain to find some pain to cry about, but nothing came to mind. I felt sorry for all those women. Some years later they felt sorry for me when the truth finally came out.

Little did I know that my time was coming. You can't keep up the façade forever.

It has been more than twenty years since that day, and I can tell you, I've felt the pain. I feel the pain, and many times I've wondered where the happiness went. I had been so busy being a perfect ATI mom with a fake smile plastered on my face that I had never allowed myself to be vulnerable and human. I never once talked to anyone about my deepest heart concerns and other issues in my life. The problems were there when I thought I had no pain, but I was unwilling to admit them and to talk about them. But sometimes when I was alone, I cried out to God to change me so that my marriage would be better and to try to understand why my parents didn't want to come visit us.

After my divorce I dared to talk about my feelings and my anguish. When I found myself alone in the house, I felt the depths of my pain as I cried until I was hoarse, and I remembered the retreat where I thought I was exempt from life's pain and misery.

Back then I was afraid to show up and really experience my life in all its messy glory and humanity. It would be too ugly. I was afraid to show up and be real, even if that would have been much easier than hiding under false pretenses. In my frame of reference, my personal pain was just that: personal, and I wasn't allowed to talk to other people about it.

Today I can tell you that the pain in my life has made me a better person-- not that I would willingly have signed up for the pain of divorce, loss, shame, guilt and suffering that has been a part of my life since that long ago day at the retreat. As I have gone through the steps of healing from my past, I often remember the day I was so proud and smug that I thought nothing painful could ever happen to me. I have to say that I like my raw self much better than my candy-coated self.

13

The Incredible Self-Effacing Woman

Living in Quebec, a predominantly French speaking province, as an English person wasn't always easy. Outside the house, I wasn't able to express myself in French as I could in English. In the beginning, I couldn't have a heart-to-heart conversation or a close friend to confide in. No one knew the real me. Because of this kind of isolation, I lost the fun loving, free spirit that I used to be, and ended up so lonely and submitted that I started to forget who I was.

Submission was always something I thought of as in sex games where there is a submissive and a dominant or training your dog into submission to you as his master. Breaking a horse also comes to mind. But as a wife, to be submitted to my husband? How does that work? Quite early in my marriage I found out. We lived by the 'umbrella of protection' schema: The husband was the head, or umbrella, covering the wife and children and protecting them from Satan's fiery darts; in effect, he was the spiritual head as well as the provider and protector of the family. This was instilled in me from the start by my ex as well as by the seminar teachings. As my Christianity was learned through the lens of these seminars, I knew nothing else.

Since our lives were dictated by what the bible had to say on a matter, this scripture became the mantra of most of the men and the scourge of the women.

"Wives submit yourselves to your husbands, as unto the Lord. For the husband is the head of the wife...therefore as the church is subject unto Christ, so let the wives be to their own husbands in everything." Ephesians 5:22-24

    When we came home from our honeymoon and my new husband made his proclamation about my body and submitting, it was the beginning of 21 years of what I understood later to be sexual abuse and feeling that I would never be able to measure up. Like a horse, I was gradually broken until I didn't know myself anymore. It wasn't a great beginning to our marriage, to say the least. To say I was surprised would be an understatement. Shocked comes closer, but really it made me a little fearful. I wasn't quite sure what it all meant, but I was about to find out. I mean, I could try to please him, but I was still my own person, wasn't I?

    Once we were separated and I started telling my story to other people, they told me that I was abused. Imagine, I never knew I was experiencing abuse until I sought counseling when the marriage was over. I had thought that in submitting I was being a good wife, but I didn't understand why that made me unhappy. I tried to please my husband, but it seemed that whatever I did, I never was good enough in his eyes. He wanted me to be a slut in the bedroom and dress like a puritan outside the bedroom. I just couldn't do that because it wasn't me, neither the slut part nor the puritan part. This was totally incongruent with the life we had chosen to live.

Once I agreed to go to a sex shop in Montreal with him to find something to wear that he would like. We made our way through the vibrators, the dildoes, the potions and lubricants until we came to the clothing, if you could call it that. We finally settled on some filmy outfit that had fake furlike stuff on the edges to try on. Honestly, when I looked in the mirror with that thing on me, I felt anything but sexy. I looked like a slut and my husband agreed that we shouldn't buy it. I don't know what specifically he was looking for, but that wasn't it, and he never brought it up again. The thing is, people buy things at sex shops to enhance their relationships and maybe to play-act, and it's done in a spirit of complicity and fun. This was anything but fun, and because of the conditioning and brain washing, I felt guilty that I couldn't please him. A normal person would have left as soon as the obsession became clear.

The stress was complete. I had diarrhea every Sunday on the way to church for the fourteen years we were in ATI. At the time I had no idea why that was. We had a half hour drive to church and often would have to stop a couple of times for me to go to the bathroom. And then once we arrived at church, I would make a dash for the ladies' room there. Interestingly, once my husband left me, the diarrhea also left me.

I felt used, good for only one thing. I cried out to God frequently to change me, but He never did. What I didn't understand until afterwards was that maybe it wasn't me that needed changing. It was true that while we were dating, my husband had asked me to not wear anything sheer or even a vee neck top, saying that because I was short, taller people (men) would be able to look down my shirt.

"No one is allowed to look down your shirt except me", he said.

Mistaking his control for love and caring, I did as he asked. But it felt as if all my hopes, dreams, individuality, and the very essence of me were being sucked out of my heart. My husband made many other demands on me, and I tried to do everything to please him, thinking that would make a good marriage. I wasn't happy but didn't really know why. I guess I just thought I was a discontented person. I learned that being a submitted wife meant that I was to happily give in to all my husband's wishes, desires, wants, needs, and demands, whether that was in the kitchen, the bedroom or anywhere else. Whether I felt like it or not.

This system of Patriarchy we had gotten ourselves into really was kinder to the men and boys than to the women. I mean, the husband and father was the boss, and he made the decisions. My role as the wife was to school the children, prepare the meals, delegate the housework, and in general, to take care of things inside the house. In addition to being submitted to him, I was to reverence my husband, defer to him in all things and to never speak a negative word about him.

No matter what I thought about an issue, he was the final authority, so he was the one to make the decisions. I could give my input, but the final decision was his. Being submitted also meant that I was to defer to my husband in all things. If he wanted the floral wallpaper and I wanted the stripes, we would have the flowers. If he wanted us to be a homeschooling family and I had reservations, we became a homeschooling family.

I became a quiet, smiling and submitted wife. I lost any sense of who I was, and my family wondered where the fun-loving and mischievous person I used to be had gone. My smile was ever pasted on even though there was much to be sad about, because we were taught that

"...a sad countenance is a public rebuke to your husband."

I understood this to mean that If people saw that I was sad, it was a reflection on him and his ability to keep me happy and content.

I often wondered why he could dress the way he wanted but I had to wear modest, long, and shapeless dresses, and why he could express himself and his wishes, but I should remain silent because

"It is better to live in a corner of a roof, than in a house with a contentious woman."

Sometimes I felt brain dead and useless because my creative, bubbly self had been squashed. I felt the pain of it every single day. There was no one to talk to about it because we were taught to

"Never give a bad report."

This basically meant that I could praise my husband for the good stuff, but I could never talk to anyone about the troubling things in my marriage, my fears and concerns or anything else.

At our annual homeschooling seminars in Knoxville, Tennessee we were taught that the back beat in contemporary rock music was evil, and we were to get it out of our home. Even Christian rock music. We gave away all the music album collections from our youth and instead we listened to Baroque classical music or hymns. That was it. However, feeling a bit rebellious, I did keep a couple of CDs of my beloved Newfoundland music. Surely God would not take me away from my roots?

One day when my children were very young, I had my son in my arms and put on some Newfoundland music. It was quite boisterous and upbeat with the accordion and fiddle. We twirled and danced around the kitchen, having a grand ole time, shrieking and laughing our heads off. And then my husband came up the stairs from his lower-level chiropractic clinic and asked me to turn off the music because

"That's not Godly music!"

And of course, any music that could stir up any semblance of lack of control or fun emotions was not of God. I didn't say anything, couldn't say anything, but obediently turned off the music and returned to whatever chore I had been doing before the fun interlude, defeated.

Why didn't I stand up to him? Why did I turn off my music? I had been so conditioned by this time, totally dependent on my husband and in a submission role for so many years that turning it off was the only thing to do. I have no idea what might have happened if I had stood up for myself. It just never occurred to me. Male headship, or patriarchy is just another form of bullying. Usually when you stand up to a bully, they back down, but I didn't know that yet.

Ever the optimist I felt that I could make the most of my confusing life, but in effect, I had traded my dreams for a false sense of security. Sure, my physical needs were being met, we had a nice home and three great sons and lots of money, but I became a joyless, constipated, prunes-and-all-bran type of person. And no one on the outside knew. It was a very lonely existence.

I never spoke to anyone about what was troubling in my marriage because that would be giving a bad report. I put up a good front and loyally supported my husband in all things. But at times when I visited family in Newfoundland, glimpses of who I really was came to the front, especially if I went there alone. The jokes would start as well as the lighthearted joie-de-vivre. My father used to say, "Everyone loves Chrissie." My smile would come back, the genuine one. I used to think it was because I loved being in Newfoundland but that wasn't it. I had lost sight of who I was at the core, and it came out when I was with my extended family.

Back in Quebec, as the years passed and I became more and more engrained in this 'new way of life', I didn't know what I wanted anymore, and I became a person who couldn't make a decision on her own, even on what piece of clothing to buy. I was afraid to express an opinion and was very unsure of myself. I had lost my self-confidence and lived by rules and regulations, all under the banner of a distorted sense of Christian submission.

One day we had Pastor Marius and his wife Elizabeth come for supper. Lively conversation ensued during and after the meal, and we all had a good time. However, a few years later when my marriage had ended and I went to Marius for some guidance, he told me that when he and Elizabeth had come for supper that time, they noticed that I didn't say anything that evening without first looking to my husband. They said it appeared as if I was looking for approval or permission to say what I did. My life on the outside was incongruent with who I really was on the inside. Sadly, during all this time, my children never knew the real me. Heck, I didn't know the real me anymore.

This kind of life was very isolating. My true life was a secret; patients from the clinic, my family, and church friends thought we were the perfect little family, so happy all the time. I was the self-effacing woman-- the one who had lost where she came from, lost her desires and creativity, and became what was expected of her. Little did those other people know what was hiding behind that long dress and false smile, complete with the requisite long hair, pinned back just so. Sometimes it hurts more to tell secrets than it is to keep them. It's hard to talk about the brokenness, the pain, and the messy parts of life that outsiders can't see.

I've made mistakes; many of them. I have regrets and sometimes I wish I could go back and do things differently. It hurts. And yet, acknowledging the truth of pain is the first step to healing from it.

14

I'm Too Holy for My Church

We attended a mildly Pentecostal church in Dorval, Quebec prior to getting into the Advanced Training Institute. I loved that church and made a lot of friends there whom I continue to be in contact with to this day. However, as we got into ATI and started living by 'biblical principles', we became more and more alienated from the church and our friends because much of what went on there was contrary to the new things we were learning as a home educating, ATI family. For example, most of the music played in the church was rock music according to ATI standards and therefore not suitable for us. The basic rock beat is 4/4, so you count 1-2-3-4. And to create the rock rhythm, you have to place the emphasis on the offbeats, which are 2 and 4. So it goes like this: one, **TWO**, three, **FOUR**.

During that time, I grew to dislike rock music, considering it to be evil, and I judged the church and its citizens for enjoying it so much. Since most of the music was played in the first half hour of the service, we started arriving late so that we wouldn't have to subject ourselves to the rock beat. It wasn't long before the pastor mentioned that we were disrupting the service by constantly coming in late. We heard about other ATI families in other congregations who would leave the sanctuary during a 'rock beat' praise song and then come back in if there was a hymn being sung. I think this drew more attention to our differences rather than the family being a 'good example' to our Christian brothers and sisters. One student's sarcastic observation was that a "large, floral-jumper- or navy-suit-clad family parading in and out of church to avoid the back beat in the music is a definite testimony of God's principles at work in your life". We just couldn't see it.

    As far as Sunday School and Youth Group were concerned, our children did not attend, the assumption being that they could be corrupted even from within the church. What if a stranger attended and showed our children a different side of life than the sheltered one they were living? There would probably be immodestly dressed young women at youth group that could corrupt my pure sons. 'Immodest' to an ATI student was a young woman wearing tight jeans, a vee neck shirt or a short skirt. And God forbid that they would make friends with young people of the opposite sex and possible dating would happen, since ATI students were supposed to be committed to courtship, meaning there would be no dating. My boys were told to 'avert their eyes' if they saw an immodestly dressed woman so that they could save their eyes for their future wives. Since the way most females dressed didn't meet up to our standards, they were constantly looking down, or out the window, or up to the sky.

   Our children were insulated from everything and everyone outside the family unit. It made me sad afterwards when I saw many young adults meet their future spouses in the church youth group, and who then went on to have happy, successful marriages.

Because we were protecting our children, on Sunday mornings they had to sit with us in the sanctuary while others their age went downstairs for some fun stories, games, and crafts. I had to make up some activity bags to occupy them during the sermon, which was usually too boring for young children. It just made more work for my already overly busy life. When they were older and all the other young people in the church were making friends and going on retreats and camping as an extension of the youth group, my children stayed at home with us. Sometimes we invited another homeschooling family over and played games and it was always fun, but I often had the nagging feeling that I was doing my boys a disservice by keeping them at home.

I wondered if what we were doing was the best thing for our children. The other young people looked like they were having a lot more fun than my kids. Having them at home all the time also made more work for me and further alienated our family from the church. But we thought we knew better than the church what was good for our children. As parents, we had ultimate control, trusting no one else with our children and their precious lives, except another ATI family, of course.

The way we dressed made us stand out, and not in a good way. On Sunday mornings my boys and husband were usually clothed in dress pants with shirts and ties. Their shirts were always tucked into their perfectly pressed pants that hovered over their perfectly shined shoes. I always wore a long dress or jumper, usually with a floral pattern. That was the standard outfit for ATI moms. Daughters could also wear a calf length, navy A-line skirt with no slit and a white blouse buttoned to the top with a little scarf at the neck to draw attention to their countenance. Along with the other two ATI families, we were the only ones in the church dressed like that. I often wished I could just haul on a comfy pair of jeans and a sweater and be myself, but I couldn't.

Because we looked and acted differently from the rest of the church, we were quite noticeable. These days I can spot a patriarchal, ATI homeschooling family a mile away, just by the way they are dressed and how they act toward each other. It all seems phony and contrived now.

Our family was different from the people in our church on so many levels, it wasn't long before we absolutely didn't fit in. We were the outsiders, the rebels, the strange ones. Eventually we found a family just to the south of us in Vermont who had a house church with homeschooling families. They weren't in ATI, so we thought we were just a little bit better than them. They had started house churching because they didn't fit in to their local church, just like us and for many of the same reasons. Their leader, a man named Mike, had been asked to leave the church with his family because he vocalized his different views once too often. House church meant that they did church at home, away from the protection of the organized church.

Believing that we had found kindred spirits, we drove to Vermont to spend a weekend with our new friends and to learn about what they were doing for church. There were five families, and they took turns having church in each family's home. We learned all the finer points of what this new way of doing church was all about.

There's a bible verse in 1 Timothy chapter 2 that talks about women "…with all submissiveness are to remain quiet in the church." That was taken to mean that during house church the women could not say one word. It goes without saying that the children did not speak either. The men took turns preparing and giving a sermon and then they discussed it, while the women and children just sat there and listened, as if they had no opinion or anything useful to say. We decided that this would be a good thing for our family, especially since we were becoming more and more different from our Lakeshore friends.

There were another two families who joined us and all together we were sixteen people. We took turns hosting church, and the men took turns preaching. One week we did church in the morning and the next week we did it late afternoon and shared a pot luck meal together afterwards. We had family communion at our house church. Each family would huddle together and confess their sins to each other before partaking of the pieces of bread and little cups of grape juice. If there were no sins to confess, we thought that the person was hiding something. I think that sometimes my sons would make up something to confess just to get it over with. Everything had to be so proper.

One Sunday we had a visiting family from Vermont at the house church. The service was following its usual order and during a quiet time of prayer, one of the very young children farted. Just like a trumpet, he farted out of his diaper and into the silence, and no one laughed. There were smirks, but not a sound. And the poor mom (me) whose child did that was mortified.

Many people outside our home church circle criticized us for isolating ourselves even further than before, but we felt we were doing the right thing. We thought that the organized church was becoming too much of a bad influence on our family. They said that there should be no 'lone rangers' where church was concerned. And where would we pay tithe? And to whom would we be accountable? And how would our children be socialized? These were all valid questions to which we thought we had all the answers. We gave to the charity of our own choosing instead of supporting a bricks and mortar church and paying a pastor. We said that we were accountable to God and that our children were socialized with other homeschooling families. That satisfied us but not our friends and family. My parents constantly worried about us.

The isolation was complete for the whole family, except for my husband who met all kinds of people each day at work. Sometimes I thought that this was best because we were well protected from all the evils of the world, even the church. Imagine, we were too holy for our church and too holy for our friends and extended family. Self-righteousness is not a good thing for anyone. I think of a song by Right Said Fred, called I'm too Sexy.

My song was I'm too Holy:

I'm too holy for my church.
Too holy for my church.

So holy it hurts.
And I'm too holy for my friends.
Too holy for my friends.
Where will it ever end?

15

Guilt and Gas Fireplaces

Whenever I smell wax crayons I think of my younger self and that box of Crayola crayons containing 8 or 24 or 64 crayons. And when I hear Johnny Cash singing "Hurt", it reminds me of a relationship I once had with a JC fan. Isn't it interesting how a smell, or a song or the sight of something can bring us back to another period in our lives? Sometimes the feeling is so strong that the emotions felt at that time long ago are brought back to the present. They are called emotional memories and can evoke love, joy, grief or fear, among others.

Gas fireplaces have that effect on me. It's not that I've ever had a love of gas fireplaces, and the in this case the fireplace was not even lit. But gas fireplaces tend to bring me back to a bright August morning in 2004.

That was the summer I was sick with mononucleosis, and I wondered where on earth I had gotten it. I had been suffering from fever and terrible headaches for a couple of weeks and had convinced myself that the doctor was going to tell me I had brain cancer. When she told me I had mononucleosis I was dumbfounded. How do you get mono when you're in a monogamous relationship? At 51 years old?

It was also the summer I took my youngest son to Newfoundland for two weeks in an attempt to reconnect with family and to have some peace. I had always prayed for peace in my life, but homeschooling our three boys, and my husband's demands as well as his chiropractic clinic in the house made sure I never had it. My son and I had the best time in St. John's! I reconnected with my family, and he got to know his cousins. We had a huge Lebanese dinner with my cousins, parents, and visiting cousins from the States. We went to the beach several times. In fact, there is a framed photo of my brother, my niece and I walking on the beach at Port Lance in the fog that still hangs in my office. A beautiful memory of a wonderful day! We came home relaxed and happy. My son had lots of stories to tell of the good times we had in Newfoundland. My mono was just about finished, I was rested, and I was now ready to get back into 'the grind'.

But that was before a particularly sunny August morning, a couple of weeks later. My personal D-day if you will. The good times of our Newfoundland visit faded into memory in the coming weeks with what was about to happen.

Sometimes certain events in life become dividing lines. There is life before the event and life after the event. Your way of life as well as your reality becomes completely different after the event. It could be a death, a move, a divorce, or job loss, but looking back, you can see that life was never the same afterwards. That's what happened to me in the summer of 2004.

I'd never have willingly signed up for what the next few years would bring, and it was a good thing I couldn't see into the future.

I remember as if it were yesterday. My husband and three sons were supposed to go with some friends for a day of paintball, leaving me home alone. But he was acting strangely that morning, like he had something on his mind that he was nervous about. He was agitated, and while the boys got ready for a great day out, he paced to and fro in his pyjamas. I hated those pyjamas because he tucked the top into the bottom and looked ridiculous with his belly protruding. I didn't know what was wrong with him; why wasn't he getting ready?

Finally, he made his announcement.

"Ok guys, you're going to have to make your way to paintball without me today because I'm not feeling so well."

He looked fine to me apart from his flustered demeanor and the pacing.

The boys' disappointment was palpable, but they made plans to go without their dad.

As for me, I was disappointed because I had been looking forward to an unstructured and peaceful day at home. And now I could see it slipping away. My heart fluttered and then sank with dread at having to cater to my husband that day. When the children were finally gone, he turned to me. I had no idea what was coming.

"I need to talk to you about something important. Something big. Something that could change our lives forever."

I couldn't imagine what that might be. My husband was often melodramatic and so I tried to take it in stride, although I sensed there was really something wrong because he couldn't look me in the eyes. Guilt has a way of doing that and I wondered what he had done now.

"We need to sit down and talk in my office."

That sounded official. His clinic office was in the basement of our beautiful home.

I wondered what could have made him so upset and mysterious.

Once, I read about a woman whose doctor wanted to see her in his office about some test results. Fearing the worst, she gave herself time to breathe, put on her best outfit and made sure her hair and makeup were impeccable. She said she did that because whatever the doctor had to say, she wanted to feel composed and to keep her dignity and humanness in the face of something that could be inhuman. Troublesome news can suck the reality and feeling out of you.

Thinking that there was nothing good going to come out of my husband's office that morning, I decided that I would do the same as that woman. I got dressed, wondering what he had to say that could be so life changing. I put on my makeup and did my hair as if I was going somewhere special. I thought about his health or whether or not he was up to something. Did he lose a lot of money? He had often dabbled in short selling on the stock market. That must be it. He had lost money.

I went down to the office where he was waiting for me. The office was beautifully decorated in mahogany woodwork and pale aqua paint. There was a gas fireplace on one side with a mahogany-colored mantel and some brass surrounding the flame pit. It took on a human quality to me as I entered the office. It was as if the fireplace was a third person in the room. My husband sat in his leather swivel desk chair, and I sat in the patients' chair, as if for an interview. The cold gas fireplace at our side was witness to his confession about the affair and that he wanted to be with the other woman whose name was Karine. Apparently, she was someone he used to know in high school and he'd recently reconnected with her. He had dated her a couple of times back then, but her mother made sure nothing came of it. When he had gone to Alberta to work, all his correspondence to Karine were intercepted and destroyed. But that was then. Now they were talking and planning.

Nothing could have prepared me for this. As I felt the life draining from my head to my toes, he told me that he wanted to spend time with her to see whether he would stay with me or go to be with her. He had been with her when I was in Newfoundland with our youngest son. I could see my marriage going up in flames. My heart pounded. My mouth went so dry I could barely swallow. And I was numb. I had absolutely nothing to say.

Guilt was written all over his face as he told me all about his new love interest, as if I was supposed to agree with him and empathize with him. He finished his speech on his knees crying at my feet, my frozen feet. I thought of my mononucleosis and wondered what his head was doing in my lap. It could have been a scene from a movie, the gas fireplace witnessing this distraught couple in such an emotional position, he with his guilt and I with my grief and shock.

At about that moment I had two distinct thoughts: First, I thanked God for giving me a way out of my troubled marriage, and second, my husband must be bipolar, and this could be just another one of his emotional outbursts.

Seriously, I thought that the man was losing it. He had always had to have a "thing", something to make him different from everyone else. At various times, he was into solving the Rubik's cube, short selling on the stock market, spiritual gifts, skiing the Rockies, Asian wife, Barleygreen, veganism, you name it. And when he was into each of these things, he talked about nothing else, and won a lot of people over to his way of thinking. You could say he was charismatic. So, when he decided that he didn't want me anymore and that he was drawn to this other woman, there was no force on the earth that would have convinced him otherwise. In his own words a few years later, "It was like a tsunami coming, coming."

    I stood up, picked up my purse, and since I was already dressed and made up, I went to Sears where it was Super Saturday and spent $400 on blankets and pillows. On this day that changed my life forever, I shopped, all the while wondering if the "true confession" in the office had really happened. To say I was numb would be an understatement. I had the feeling that I was somewhere else watching myself go through the motions of looking at things in the store, chatting with people I ran into, and wondering how on earth I was going to get through this nightmare.

    I was more worried about the logistics of it all than about losing my husband. My heart had grown so cold and numb with the specifics of our marriage, it had been years since I had stopped crying, and I didn't cry on that day either.

    In the following days, I discussed the whole situation with my mother. She had always been very accommodating with our way of life even if it mystified her. However, she had blamed my husband for bringing me and my family down this path of self-righteousness, patriarchy and isolation. I'll never forget what she said to me one day, before divorce had ever been mentioned.

"Christine, I've always been against divorce, but you can divorce him with my blessing."

I couldn't believe that my very Catholic mom would say such a thing. I guess it just drove home to me how concerned she had been all those years about our way of life. And that's when I knew that my parents, brother and sisters would stand behind me no matter what happened.

16

Getting Through the Daze

"Christine, what have you been doing these days?"

"Oh, I've been quite busy rocking in my rocking chair, cooking eggs and vacuuming up cat hair. I've been losing weight as well. In fact, I'm now at my goal weight. How about you?"

I was becoming the invisible woman, you know, the one who is afraid to go out of the house and who feels like she's nothing without a husband by her side.

After that memorable day in my husband's office, it took me about six weeks to realize that my marriage was really over. No amount of crying, wailing and howling was going to save it. It didn't occur to me that it wasn't worth saving if he already had someone else. You might be thinking that with all the things that went on in my life, I'd be happy he was leaving. I came to be happy later on, but at that time I had no idea how I would live without a husband. Change is difficult.

Since he was already seeing someone else, I asked him to move out. I didn't really ask him; I told him he couldn't come home after he went to see his new girlfriend. I remember Thanksgiving weekend that year. My sister had come to spend the time with us, but my husband left for Trois Rivieres to see 'her', saying that he would be back for the turkey dinner on Sunday. I was frantic, couldn't see straight, and my heart would not stop pounding. I didn't think I was going to be able to cook a turkey with all that was going on, and I didn't. To this day I can't believe that I even considered doing it.

On that Thanksgiving weekend, while he was away with his new love interest, I put every trace of him in paper grocery bags and piled them in the main entrance of the house. Finally, I had a little backbone. Then I called and told him that he couldn't come back in the house, that all his things were waiting for him. Then I called a locksmith, a man from my old church, who came and changed all the locks on the house. He was so kind to come on Thanksgiving Monday and gave me an excellent price. I also had him put a one-way lock on the clinic door. I could go into the clinic, but my husband couldn't come into the house. Interestingly, I think this was the first time I asserted myself in my 21-year marriage.

Over the next days I went through photo albums and got rid of pictures of him and I, our wedding album, which by now was a farce in my eyes, and other things that reminded me of him. I did save some photos for the children. I put them in envelopes and handed them over much later.

Once I realized that it was over, I put my youngest son in school for the first time, in grade five. He later told me that's when his life began. He had felt like a nobody too. As my husband moved out, every trace of him was erased from our home. Since my older sons were already in CEGEP and university, and now my youngest was in school, I was home alone with my memories, regrets, disappointments, and grief.

Alone. I had not been alone in 21 years. Overnight I went from being a busy homeschooling wife and mother, who ran the household, cooked the meals and did the finances for her husband's business, to that catatonic woman who sat in her rocking chair by the phone. Back and forth I rocked for hours, it seemed. It had been a long time since I was alone and didn't have anything to do. Day after day I rocked in my chair, not able to focus enough to read a book nor motivated to cook or clean the house. All I did was vacuum up cat hair and cook eggs for supper. I couldn't eat and the weight was falling off me. A couple of months later I had achieved my ideal weight for the first time in my life, but it was the most difficult weight loss imaginable.

I often thought of all the other divorced women I knew who had worked throughout their marriages. They had something to do during and after their divorces. Before I was married, I was a teacher, independent and had a good salary. Now I was nothing. I had given up my teaching job to bear children and then to homeschool them and to submit to my husband. The rules of ATI were specific: women were not to work outside the home. They were to be "keepers at home". If only I had not done that, I could have had something to occupy my days. But here I was, in my rocking chair, not fit to teach anyone, anything, anymore.

I drank wine. After the children were in bed, I drank wine in my newly arranged bedroom with a bowl of cheezies at my side and reading a book with my cat, Treacle beside me. I thought the wine would help me sleep. I remember the time I awakened at 3AM. The bedside light was still on, the empty wine glass lay beside me, and Treacle was eating the leftover cheezies. I had sunk to a new low.

That fall we all got sick. My three boys broke out in chicken pox, I ended up on antibiotics for an infection and even the cat was depressed. It was as if we were all falling down a deep hole with no bottom.

Autumn had always been my favourite time of year, but as October faded into November and the leaves all fell off the trees, I could see my life slipping away. My shame at having been abandoned by my husband at 51 years old was complete. No more Proverbs 31 woman. No more denim jumpers. No homeschooling and no endless stream of people through our beautiful home. I didn't even know who I was anymore. I had been so indoctrinated into the ways of the cult and so protected from the outside world that I didn't know how to be in this world.

I remember staring out my kitchen window in despair, tears streaming down my face, truly believing that everything outside my window was evil and it made me afraid. I had a BMW, my prize car, sitting in the driveway but I was afraid to use it for anything but getting groceries that I couldn't eat anyway. I felt like my life was over and it was hard to believe that the sun still shone, children still laughed in the neighborhood, people mowed their lawns and raked leaves. Life went on for everyone else, but mine seemed to be at a standstill. I didn't know who I was anymore, and I couldn't imagine that I would ever smile again, that my heart would be light, and I would enjoy life. I didn't know how to live in this world.

    A friend offered to take me to a Christian counselor in an effort to help me find my way and make some sense of the rest of my life. I went to him six times. He walked back and forth in his office, bible in hand, spouting all the verses that told of the hell and damnation that was going to come on my husband. I wondered when he was going to get around to helping me.

How was I going to live? How would I feel whole again? When I told some of the women at my church who I was seeing, an older woman named Peggy, dropped her head, and sighed. She couldn't really say anything but later on I heard rumors that my counselor had cheated on his wife, but they were still together. At that point I realized that these sessions of bible verse spouting were not helpful, and he wasn't much of an example. I thought then, and I still do, that if someone was going to counsel me, they had to walk the walk. So, I ditched him.

    I started seeing another counselor, a non-Christian woman who listened to my story. I didn't understand at that point, what an obscure and different life I had led. Words like submission, being saved, crying out to God and the rest of the Christian jargon was like Greek to her. But that was just Christian jargon. I had gone quite beyond being an ordinary born-again Christian. To explain to another Christian what my life had been would have been daunting. But trying to tell the unindoctrinated all about our lifestyle and beliefs was no small feat, but she rose to the task of helping me. I think she was fascinated with my story and I'm sure she had never heard such things in her practice before.

Without judgment, she told me to make small changes, like changing around the furniture in the bedroom and drinking my morning coffee from a different cup. They were small and seemingly insignificant changes, but they did make me feel better and not so afraid. I don't know what I was afraid of over the next few weeks, but I was afraid. I stopped seeing that counselor when she had me lie on the floor and let it all out. I think she wanted me to shout and scream, but I couldn't get one sound out. I had been so brainwashed into keeping my feelings to myself and putting on a false front that I was unable to express myself in that way. My safety net had been broken and I was still in free fall. I didn't know when or how I would hit bottom. It was so difficult to get through the days, the long days that were no longer filled with things to do.

Most of what I did over the next few months was to continue vacuuming up cat hair, cook eggs, and rocking in my chair. By and by I realized that I was losing too much weight and I had no sense of time. It was like an out of body experience. I figured if I kept on like that, I would become sick and not be able to take care of myself or my youngest son. Around that time, I wrote a checklist of things that I had to do every day just to put some structure into my life and hopefully to help me gain some strength. They might seem insignificant to any other person, but they were about all I was able to do.

Here's what was on my list:
1. Get up, get dressed and no going back into the bedroom until bedtime.
2. Eat six times every day, even if one of those times it was just a spoonful of yogurt.
3. Go on the treadmill every day for at least five minutes. If I could do more, so much the better.
4. Go outside every day for at least ten minutes. Sometimes I just stood outside the door until the time was up.
5. Make one phone call every day, either to a friend or family member.

I wrote down the five things each morning and they had to be checked off by evening. I stuck to this list religiously and before long I started to feel a little better in body and spirit. However, I was still very much under the influence and beliefs of the cult. I was not equipped to be alone and that made me feel quite helpless. This wasn't supposed to happen. Not to an ATI family who followed all the rules.

Throughout my marriage, I hadn't filled my own car with gas, so I didn't even know what side the tank was on. The first time I went to get gas I had to do some maneuvering the car back and forth before I figured it out and filled up for the first time by myself. And when I went to the car wash it was even worse. I thought that once you entered the wash garage, the car would be magically propelled forward. So, I just sat there waiting and daydreaming. After a while I heard some car horns tooting. Looking around, I realized that they were tooting at me.

I realized that I had to put the car in gear and move it myself. I felt angry that at 51 years old I didn't know how to put the car through the car wash, and I was humiliated. When and why had I signed up to be so helpless?

I really felt that what had happened to me was my own fault. I was not good enough as a wife, a lover, a partner nor as a person. I thought I was completely unlovable and worthless. Try as I might, I just wasn't capable of being someone or something that I wasn't. And therein lay the blame squarely on my shoulders. That's what I thought.

One day the children and I were invited to supper at another ATI family's house. I felt as if we were the week's charity case, so much I was ashamed of my state in life at this point. Suddenly, I was quiet around these people whom I had known for years and had had lively conversations with. I had nothing to say, really and I felt that anything I might have said wouldn't be important to anyone anyway. I felt as if I had been erased but I was still there and I didn't know why. We ate a delicious supper to good conversation, but I just sat there eating, listening and wanting to sink through the floor, so much I felt out of place. I was having this out of body experience every time I was around our old friends.

After supper was over and the dishes were cleared up, Marissa took me aside, put her hands on my shoulders, looked me squarely in the eye and said, "Christine, this is not your fault. No matter what you believe or what he said to you, it's not your fault."

I chose to believe her, and that's one of the many things that saved me from my darkest thoughts and the shame they brought. I came to understand that there was nothing I could have done to save my marriage, that it really wasn't my fault, and that I needed to learn to take care of myself and my children. I am thankful to this day for those words of wisdom imparted to me when I needed most to hear them. In fact, I have used the same words to encourage other women who find themselves in dire marital straits.

17

A Total Cleanout

The mantra of the day is "Be Yourself" and "Be Authentically Yourself". What if you're asked to do something that feels uncomfortable for you, but it would make the other person happy, should you do it? My husband had a thing about certain kinds of underwear, and desired for me to wear certain sexy things that made me feel uncomfortable. That's the only way I can describe it. But a wife was supposed to reverence (that awful word again) her husband and do everything he wanted, so I went out frequently and bought things that he might like. I didn't like them. I felt uncomfortable in them, and this kind of clothing was incongruent with the way I had to dress the rest of the time. Wearing them made me feel ashamed of my womanhood and not wearing them made me feel that I was disrespecting my husband.

Once the marriage was over, I started making small changes. Once I had changed the furniture around and started drinking my coffee from another cup, it was time for the underwear. I took a big garbage bag and started going through the dresser drawers and bedroom closet. I started throwing things in the bag: thongs, lacy things, filmy things and uncomfortable things. I didn't stop until the drawers were empty, and the bag was full. I put the bag out to the street, never to darken my drawers or body again. Even then, I felt guilty for throwing those things out. I don't know why I felt guilty. My husband was never coming back so he would never know about my ruthless cleanout. But still.

My husband had never liked the cotton nighties I loved to wear. He thought they looked puritan. Now the time had come to get some pyjamas that I wanted to wear and that I would be comfortable in. It was time to please myself, not someone else. That wasn't being selfish, was it? For the next year I tried but was not able to buy myself sleepwear. I would go to Sears or la Senza and bring several selections to the dressing room. But I could only see myself through my ex-husband's eyes, and I would start to cry, right there in the dressing room. It was a long time before I was able to buy myself some sleep wear that I liked without feeling judged and ashamed. Thankfully I got over that when my friend told me that her husband loves her and thinks she's beautiful even if she's in an old t shirt with holes and stains. I couldn't imagine.

18

Tears And Some Good Advice

Once I had secured the mildewed Y2K money in my own bank account, I had some decisions to make. But I couldn't make them. It felt as if any decision I made about any area of my life, I had to run it by my husband, who I hadn't yet started calling my 'ex'. In fact, depositing the $30 000 in the bank was the first time I ever asserted myself and defied him. Making decisions was not my forte, and that was an understatement. I'm not sure, but I don't think that in the 21 years I was married that I ever made and executed an important decision on my own.

But now I was on my own and I quickly realized that if I didn't decide what to do, there was no one there to decide for me. My family in Newfoundland saw my marriage breakup as a golden opportunity for two things. First, they figured that since 'the man' was gone, I could return to my Catholic roots. I tried to explain to them that my children never knew Catholicism because they had all been born into born-again Christianity. All our social and emotional support came from the church that we had attended for many years before house churching. So that wasn't going to happen. Secondly, they thought I could now return to my other roots and move back to Newfoundland.

Roots. I didn't know who I was any more. Was I the girl who was raised by Catholic parents in Newfoundland, went to university in Nova Scotia and did strange things, like reciting "The Night of the King's Castration" on snowbanks in winter? Was I the teacher of young children in Alberta, the girl who skied every weekend and had lots of friends? Or was I the French speaking, born-again Christian woman who homeschooled and spanked her children and submitted to her husband? I just didn't know any more. I didn't know what I wanted, and I didn't know who I was.

My family was so excited at the prospect of having me back in Newfoundland and I was excited to go, until one of my children declared that he was going to stay in Quebec. That changed things majorly. Meanwhile time was marching on, and I had to decide. I didn't want to further break up my family.

We used to attend a little Church in Deux Montagnes before getting into ATI. At that point we became too holy for that little church and went elsewhere. But now I had a yearning to go back there because it was small and only five minutes from home. I was welcomed with open arms by all my old friends who were still there, Mary, Sue, Michelle, Cynthia, and others.   Still wearing my wedding rings (because who was I without wedding rings?) I sat crying alone in my pew at the end of the service. I had never been a person who expressed a lot of emotion in front of others, but this time I just couldn't help it. A sweet lady in front of me turned around and asked me what was wrong. I told her that my husband had just left me, and I didn't know what to do. I told her I didn't understand why he left. I had tried so hard to be a good wife, but it was all for naught. Darlene became a close friend after that because we had a lot in common. She had been in the same situation a few years prior and she was able to read between the lines about what had really been wrong with my marriage.

By this time, I was really blubbering, and Michelle came over with the same question. I told her about my marriage and how my family wanted me to move back to Newfoundland, but I was torn because of the son who wanted to stay in Quebec. I told her I didn't know where to begin because everything was so hard. Michelle took me by the shoulders and gave me some advice I've never forgotten.

"Christine, it's not time for you to move to Newfoundland. When it is the right time, it will be easy."

I chose to follow her advice and made the decision to start looking for a house in Deux Montagnes. I knew Michelle had given me good advice because once I decided to stay in Quebec for the time being, things got easier. I couldn't tell you how many times I've echoed Michelle's words to other people who are trying hard to make something work but keep coming up against obstacles. God, or the Universe is trying to make a point.

19
Moving Day

My ex wanted to keep the house because of the clinic in the basement, so he bought me out, which was what I wanted. I couldn't have imagined staying in that house with all the memories. I needed to start anew. Once that part was settled, I started looking for a house for my sons and me. I wasn't in any kind of mood to go looking for a house, but I did have a few criteria:

1. The house had to be of recent construction, within the previous five years because I didn't want to have expensive repairs.
2. It had to be within walking distance to the commuter train so that my boys could easily make their way to Montreal for cegep and university.
3. It had to have at least three bedrooms. Four would be great.
4. The house had to be completely finished, top to bottom, and
5. I had to be able to pay cash for it.

I hired a real estate agent and together we managed to find exactly what I needed. After viewing many houses and duplexes over a couple of weeks, I found it. You know the feeling when you put your hand on the doorknob, open it and you just know that this is the perfect house for you? That's what happened. The house had not three, but four bedrooms, the basement was finished, it was close to the commuter train and within my budget. So, my children and I prepared to move to 1509 Ovila Forget in Deux Montagnes.

Packing up the house was something I was just not able to do. Some dear friends came over several times to pack boxes and help me to throw things away. I don't know how I would have managed without them. We went through the house deciding what would stay for my ex who would be moving back into the house, and what I would take with me.

Moving day arrived on a sunny but cold day in February that year. It had been only four months since I had asked my husband to leave. People from my church came to help with the move. There were about twelve of them. Paul rented a U haul truck; Charlene stayed behind to clean the house from top to bottom, and others waited at the new house to set up the beds and other furniture. I had a special piano mover to move that heavy but delicate piece of furniture.

As people were loading the truck, I wandered around, not sure what I should do. I remember being quite on edge, and sad because this was not a joyful move for me. Life as I knew it would never be the same again. I didn't realize it at the time, but that wasn't such a terrible thing.

I had a very large, very heavy roll top desk that had to be moved in two pieces: the upper part with the roll and drawers, and the lower part that housed the filing drawers. It was made of cherry wood and was a treasured item for me. My ex had made it for me many years prior. I watched as five men coordinated taking the desk apart to put in the truck.

And that was when I lost it. My life for the past 21 years flashed before my eyes, which were now brimming with tears. I felt claustrophobic and had to leave the house because I was about to have a horrible meltdown. All the stress of the past few months came to the surface when I saw my friends doing their darndest to take care of me. I walked out of the house that day and did not return to it for several years. I ended up at the grocery store, going up and down the aisles with nothing really to buy; it was just something to do. Finally, I picked up some paper plates and disposable cutlery because someone was bringing food.

By the end of the day the move was complete. The beds were made, the furniture placed, and everyone had eaten. I couldn't imagine how I would ever survive in this house with no husband, but I did, and it was fine. It was just that my mindset from the ATI years was very much present and the shame I felt at my divorce knew no bounds. My umbrella of protection had been taken away and I was all alone. Now I would be the one making the decisions, paying the bills, supporting my children, and just trying to survive as a single mom. At 52 years old.

Ovila Forget was a long street with most of the houses identical and most of them filled with young French families. And in all that sameness I finally felt safe, incognito, free to do nothing, if that's what I wanted. And that little house filled all our needs, my boys and me.

We lived there for five years during which time my older boys eventually moved out and got places of their own, and I spent my time substitute teaching and frequenting dating sites to find that very necessary husband. In fact, I secretly believed that my full-time job now was to find a husband. I truly believed that I was nothing without a man at my side. Thankfully I don't feel that way anymore.

Back in the old house there was a closet in a spare bedroom that had been completely cleaned out except for one thing: my wedding dress and veil from a happier time some twenty-one years prior. Did I really want my wedding dress in my new house? What do you do with a wedding dress from a broken marriage? So, I left it there.

The sun shining through the window that day showed my dress hanging there in a forgotten light, dust motes floating in the air. My wedding dress that had symbolized so much to me-- love, commitment, family, a future, sitting there in the sun filled room, mocking me. My dress and veil cascading to the floor in the empty closet in the empty room echoed the emptiness in my heart. Not long after the move, my ex-husband called to tell me that he had 'found' my wedding dress in the closet and asked me what I wanted him to do with it. I told him he could burn it and hung up.

20

Divorce Fudge

Yes, you read that right. Divorce Fudge saved me. It is one of the humorous parts of my life during those twilight years between cult, divorce and healing. In fact, Divorce Fudge continues to heal me and give me confidence many years later.

One year after my husband and I separated and I had moved into my little house on Ovila Forget, Deux Montagnes. I wanted a divorce. There was no getting around it, I was going to be a divorced woman whether I liked it or not. I needed to move on, have financial protection and a bit of a plan for my life. Off I went to the lawyer to get the thing started. I hadn't realized it would be so complicated and costly.

As visits to my lawyer intensified, so did the lawyer's bills. I already was receiving some alimony and child support from my ex, but with all the expenses of moving and helping my older children in university, I was coming up short on the financial side of things. I sat in my rocking chair in my new house day after day, wondering how on earth I was going to pay all the bills. I figured that if I had gotten this far, God wasn't going to leave me flat now. The $30 000 I had taken to the bank on that October day now was a part of the 'family patrimony'. In Quebec, everything that was gained during the marriage is split down the middle. That meant all our assets were listed, and since we had no debts, the assets were split down the middle. But before all that was settled, I needed ready money to pay the bills.

One October day in 2005, I was talking to a friend about my financial concerns. I told her about my legal bills and discussed with her some options for paying them. My heart was so heavy I couldn't see straight, let alone find a way to come up with the money. My friend suggested that I sell my fudge. I hadn't thought of that.

I did have a fudge recipe that was not only foolproof but was well loved by everyone who knew me and had tasted it. I was sure that the fudge would sell but there was no way I was going to put myself out there to drum up business. I told her that selling the fudge was a mountain too big for me to climb. I could make the fudge but that was all. There was no way I felt able to advertise, promote and then deliver the fudge to customers. I was living with too much shame and stress at that point, and my confidence was in the gutter. My happy place was at home, safe from the world. And people.

My dear friend Barbara offered to take orders for my fudge, collect the money and then have people come to her house to pick it up. I couldn't believe the magnitude of what she was about to do for me. She told me to make a sample of the finished product and a plate of samples for her to pass around. So, I did just that. Barbara took samples of my fudge everywhere she went and took orders. She approached the cashier at Zellers, the teller at her bank, her car mechanic and all her friends and family. They all loved my fudge! I had asked her to tell the people that I would make all the fudge the first week of December that year and deliver it to her place.

While Barbara took orders, I gathered my ingredients and waited. Every other day she would call me with ten orders or twenty orders or eight orders. My notebook was filling up and the calls kept coming until one day I realized that with all those fudge sales I would have enough money to pay my lawyer. It's funny but at about the same time the orders stopped coming. There just wasn't another order. I didn't mind that the orders stopped; I had some work on my hands, something to occupy my mind, and there would be money coming in. You could say it was my first job, post-cult.

As promised, the first week of December I made fudge. I divided the number of orders by five, and made one fifth each day, Monday to Friday. Each order was put in a little white dish, covered with cellophane, and tied with raffia and a little Christmas decoration on top. At the end of the week, I delivered a carload of fudge to Barbara's house. She called all her people who came for their orders and paid her. She in turn, gave me the money, and I went to pay my lawyer. My gratefulness knew no bounds.

After that Christmas, I became known as the fudge lady, and I told my story to anyone who would listen. I did that so they could see that the amount of fudge I sold and the amount I had to pay the lawyer matched up. I didn't see it as a coincidence but the hand of a mighty and loving God, not to mention the love of a loyal friend.

The next autumn, people were asking if I was going to make the fudge again. Another friend, Cathy, offered to publicize it at the school board office where she worked. That brought another raft of orders, along with orders from the people who had bought from me the year before.

I decided to call it Divorce Fudge. I tell people I named it as such, not because my divorce was sweet nor because the name irks my ex, but because that fudge saved me in so many ways back when I was trying to find my way. Making the fudge paid my bills, occupied my time, and gave me a glimmer of self-confidence to build on. Since that time, I have sold Divorce fudge every year at craft shows, and people flock to my table to get some. Eventually I started selling it in little clear plastic boxes that my new husband and I call 'purse packs' because you can keep it in your purse, and it doesn't get crushed. It's just perfect for when you need some fudge, and everyone needs fudge at some time or another.

I've included my recipe in the Appendix of this book. If you follow the instructions to the letter, you will be rewarded with the best fudge in the world.

21

The Day I Forgot My Name

I glanced in the mirror one day, as I usually do when getting ready to go somewhere. Lingering, I began to study this person looking back at me, hazel eyes and serious expression.

"Who are you now?" I asked.

And as I stared some more, I started to reflect on what brought me to this place, on this street, in this town in Nova Scotia. It was a long and difficult journey back to here and back to me. I remembered growing up in Newfoundland at a time when innocence reigned, and the only technology was a telephone and two channels on the TV that went off air at 9PM.

Many years later, I went to university in Nova Scotia and fell in love with that place. However, job opportunities dictated that I move to Alberta to teach in a little town called High Prairie. There I developed my style, my moxie and a devil-may-care attitude which all served me well right up until the time I left there to marry and live in Quebec.

Suddenly who I was, was not enough anymore. I didn't realize it at the time, but I had slowly been indoctrinated into what I found out many years later was a fundamentalist cult. It had crept up so slowly on me that I didn't realize it until I was trapped in a way of life that was distasteful to my family and former friends.

"You've been through a lot", I said to the reflection in the mirror, "but you've come out stronger and with a wisdom and compassion you would never have acquired in another life."

So that's what these wrinkles and grey hair are all about.

This is one of the many stories about the first steps in my journey back to Nova Scotia and back to me.

Going through a divorce, menopause, and empty nest syndrome all at the same time lent itself to some interesting life situations. For example, not long out of the free-fall of divorce, I found myself yearning to meet new people. People who didn't know me in my former life and who would accept me for just me.

I had a friend who invited me to go to a course with her; it was good for confidence building, she said. On a cold evening in February, I found my English self in a church basement in North Montreal at the Sylva Bergeron course. There were about 70 people, all smiling and speaking in French. They wanted to shake my hand-- human touch, I thought. That's good. I couldn't remember the last time someone touched me, other than my massage therapist.

When we all sat down for the course to begin, we were told the rules: No sucking on water bottles throughout the evening; at the break there would be water and coffee-- if you didn't like that, too bad for you. The course would go on well past midnight, be brave for driving home and stop worrying about foolish things. We were not to ever talk about what brought us there or our personal problems. With growing apprehension, I sat down and wondered what on earth this was all about.

The next order of business was for us newbies to introduce ourselves. We were to stand, say our name in a voice that could be heard by all 70 people in the room, and then spell it. That doesn't sound like a difficult thing to do, but for someone who has stage fright it was a mountain. Oh, and did I mention that it was all in French? I could say my name with a French accent but to spell it in French also. How hard could it be?

As my turn approached, with heart pounding I stood and started to say my name. I started but then I got stuck. See, between Christine and Faour, there was another name, another life, my married surname, which I hadn't gotten rid of yet. I started with "Christine…"

Did you ever hear of liminal space? It's when you have left the tried and true and you haven't yet replaced it with something new. Think of a trapeze artist going from the safety of one swing to the safety of the next swing. In between the swings is the terrifying, breath-holding, heart-stopping space of 'what if'.

And there I was. Am I Christine Massicotte or Christine Faour? The time it took to decide seemed like an eternity. The room was silent. My heart pounded. Everyone was waiting for me to remember my name. And then I said it.

"Christine Faour" c-h-r-i-s-t-i-n-e   Christine
F-a-o-u-r Faour

The applause brought me back to reality. No one in the room knew what had just happened. But I did. In that instant of liminal space, I decided to take back my name and my life.

I continued with the Sylva Bergeron course for 12 more sessions. Every week there were exercises to do in front of the group, and I did them all, with gusto. The course gave me more confidence and I met some wonderful people.

But I'll never forget the day when I, just for a moment, didn't know my name.

22

It Must Be God's Will

I sat at the kitchen table, patiently sipping tea. It had been five years since my divorce was final. Music poured out of the living room, as yet another prospective buyer tried out my piano. A half hour had already passed, and it seemed as if Celeste Lemire (not her real name) had traveled all the way to Deux Montagnes just to practice on a professional piano. My piano.

"I think this will be perfect!" Celeste said, finally emerging from the living room, beaming. "You did say I could have it for $4300, right? I've been praying and I believe that it's God's will that I have this exact piano. I brought cash."

Praying, I thought. She must be a Christian.

"It's yours, Celeste. When will you have the movers come?"

"I'll arrange for them to come tomorrow. I just can't wait to have that piano in my home."

I accepted the cash in exchange for the piano, the most beautiful and treasured piece of furniture I owned. With the movers coming the next day, I could still enjoy the class and comfort it brought into my life for another twenty-four hours. Before they came, I polished the lacquered finish to a brilliant shine and then bid my Yamaha upright piano goodbye.

The next day I stood by the living room window, watching as the piano exited my home and my life. The end of an era, I thought. Craning my neck, I caught a final glimpse of the Expert Piano Movers truck making its way down Ovila Forget, getting smaller and smaller in the distance. I thought about the events that had brought the piano into my family's life eleven years earlier.

My reverie first brought me on a little trip down memory lane and the beliefs my family held back when we were in a ATI. Most people don't think of God and prayer until a catastrophe, like an accident or a deadly diagnosis happens. Then they pray hard, and they ask others to pray for them or their loved one. However, it was different for us. I remembered a scripture that said, "Pray without ceasing" and how we had taken it to heart. It was God who was in control of our lives, not us. Our friends and family had no idea how being in the cult had brainwashed us. My husband and I prayed for everything: what kind of drill to buy, where to go on vacation and when to have sex. Prayer was an integral part of our lives, as was waiting for 'promptings' from God to know if we were doing the right thing. Back then, coincidences were not coincidences; they were God's will. In hindsight, I could see how naïve we were.

We needed a piano for our son's budding music talent. He was gifted, there was no doubt about that, and he had outgrown the portable keyboard that had only three octaves. Because we believed that it was God's will for us to have a piano, we set to praying for just the right one.

"God, we're praying for you to provide us with a piano, one that will stay with us for a lifetime. Lord, you've seen our son's musical talent, and you see that the keyboard will not be useful any more for him. We're asking you for a piano in good condition, something that will add beauty and grace to our living room. Oh, and God, we have $3000 to spend."

Day after day, week after week we prayed the same prayer, trusting that God would provide the best piano for our budget. We searched the classifieds, but to no avail. We were very particular about what we wanted. Then one day there was an ad in the Montreal Gazette for an upright, lacquered Yamaha piano. That was more like it, but the asking price was $5000.

"We don't have $5000, and we asked God for a $3000 piano. This can't be God's will" I declared. "How can we pray for a $3000 piano and then go to look at a $5000 one?"

"Sometimes God works in mysterious ways", my husband said, as he prepared to call the seller.

He made arrangements to go see the piano the next day and to make sure everything would be all right, he invited his friend Art Cannoli to come along for moral support and counsel. Art had owned a music store in downtown Montreal for many years but had given up managing the shop now that he was eighty years old.

"Art has the knowledge about pianos that we don't have, and perhaps he can evaluate whether or not the piano is actually worth $5000"

"Well, I still think this is a lost cause."

"You have to trust God. If it's His will, He will make a way for us to have that piano. Just keep praying."

We arrived at an apartment in a well-tended sector of Laval. A tiny woman with blonde hair waving a cigarette welcomed us in. Her name was Marie Labonne, and she was moving to Abu Dhabi within the month. She said she would be there for three years.

On entering, I observed the tidiness of the place. Works of art including paintings and carvings from faraway places adorned the softly painted walls. Not a thing was out of place in the kitchen or the living room.

"I'm putting most of my belongings into storage" she explained, "but the piano cannot be in a place with temperature extremes, and that's why I'm selling it."

The piano was magnificent. Set against a pale blue wall with a lone silver candelabra on top, I was pretty sure that Art and my husband wouldn't find any defect that might lower the price. Since none of us could actually play the piano, we had to be content just examining and admiring it. Each of us played a few keys just to hear the sound.

"Can you play us a little tune, Marie?"

"Oh no, you wouldn't want to hear me play. I'm a complete beginner and have been taking lessons for only six months," she said shyly, taking a long haul on her cigarette. Marie was taking lessons, but I was pretty sure she had the piano more for aesthetic than practical purposes. My husband pulled the piano out from the wall and he and Art went behind it to look at the backside and soundboard. I stood back, arms folded, still skeptical.

"There's not a scratch on the lacquer. The soundboard is in perfect condition. I can find nothing wrong with this piano", Art whispered.

Reluctantly the two of them emerged from behind the piano and my better half had to admit defeat.

"Marie, this is a magnificent piano and I'm sure it is worth $5000. However, we only have $3000 to spend. I wish you all the best in finding a buyer before your move to Abu Dhabi."

The three of us stood looking wistfully at the piano before leaving. I remembered praying harder at that point. For a miracle or something.

Surprising everyone, my husband said, "Well, if you do find a buyer, can you let me know? Here's my phone number. I would really appreciate it."

"I will."

"Why on earth did you ask her that?" I hissed later in the car. "What difference does it make to us if she finds a buyer or not? We won't be buying it, that's for sure."

"You never know, Christine. God can do anything. Have a little faith."

Over the next couple of weeks, we kept looking, but it was impossible get Marie's piano out of our minds. Nothing else we saw could even come close. Earnest prayers went heavenward daily.

"Maybe we should just borrow the extra 2000$", I ventured one day.

"Well now, that wouldn't be God's will at all. We prayed for a $3000 piano and that's what we'll get. It's not God's will for us to go into debt for a piano."

We prayed harder, pleading with God.

"God, we know that it's your will for us to have a piano. Otherwise, why would you have given our son so much talent? God, we really need that piano. We would take such good care of it. Please God, make it happen."

We imagined what the piano would look like in our living room. We pictured our son playing beautiful classical pieces on it. We thirsted for a home filled with music that was pleasing to God. We wished, we coaxed, we pleaded some more, but the Almighty was silent.

"I guess it wasn't God's will for us to have that piano," my husband admitted one day. "We might as well just forget about it."

And with that, our vision for a beautiful piano died. God hadn't answered our prayer. Then, on a cold Tuesday evening when we weren't even thinking about the piano we had lost, the phone rang. I noticed an unfamiliar number on the call display.

"Hello?"

"Hi, it's Marie Labonne. Do you remember coming to see my piano last month?"

As if I could forget.

"Yes, I remember you. Weren't you leaving for Abu Dhabi around this time?"

"Oh yes, in fact the movers are coming at 8AM tomorrow morning to move my things to a storage unit, and then I'll be on my way. I never sold the piano, and your husband did give me his number, so if you can take it away before the movers come, it's yours for $3000."

We scrambled to find a piano mover for 7AM the next morning. After making several calls he found one who would come but hiked the price because of the short notice. We didn't care. We would have the piano, the one we had prayed for. There was no doubt in our minds that this was God's will.

Thinking on all these things, I continued to stare out the window long after the Expert Piano Movers had driven out of sight. I reminisced about the years of beautiful music the piano had given us. I remembered my son filling the house with works by Chopin, Bach, Beethoven, and Handel while I cooked dinner for my family and when company came over. By this time, I was crying, not just for the piano but also for the life I had lost.

God's will indeed, I thought. I asked God if it was his will that the piano had to be sold to pay the bills after my nasty divorce. I wondered if the divorce was his will as well. The empty room echoed as I said to no one in particular, "I think I am going to break up with God."

23
Dating Sites

Once I had mastered the car wash and started getting out more, I felt that I was nothing without a man at my side. In fact, I now openly told my children that my full-time job was to find another husband. I can't believe I ever said that but it's where my head was at the time. Really, I had been brainwashed to believe that a woman's life purpose was to reverence her husband and be his helpmeet, be his playmate in bed whenever he wanted, bear his children, and keep house. Even though I had graduated from university with two degrees, I believed this with all my heart. I had no idea just how I was to find this elusive husband, but I was going to give it my best effort anyway. I had a good look around my church but there were no available men there, and I had no other opportunity to meet anyone anywhere else because I didn't go anywhere.

One day a close friend told me about this website she was on where you could meet people and it was called the Christian Café. I didn't realize at the time that it was a dating site; I thought it was an online site, like an in-person coffeehouse where you could converse with people who were also Christian. So, I signed up and before long I was getting hit on by some interesting men. They all lived far away, like in the United States or Western Canada. There were virtually none from Quebec, as far as I could see. That didn't bother me too much because I wasn't ready for a relationship. I was still grieving my marriage. But once I started getting attention, I started to feel desirable again. Some people out there thought I was a good catch. Once I realized this, the Christian Café had my full attention. I put up a profile complete with a couple of good photos, showing me in a good light. My name was Treacle, and I was from "Une Petite Ville Francaise". I think I was pretty naive and looking for a romantic dream at that point. You can see how that shines through in my dating profile.

Describe the type of relationship you are looking for. What qualities would you like in this relationship or person? Are you seeking a particular age range?

"Oh, the comfort, the inexpressible comfort of feeling safe with a person, having neither to weigh thoughts nor measure words, but pouring them all out, just as they are, chaff and grain together, certain that a faithful hand will take and sift them, keep what is worth keeping, and with a breath of kindness blow the rest away."
This quote by George Eliot sums up the essence of what I am looking for in a life partner...

It's hard to put it down without creating an expectation on the other end. I would never want my man to try to fit a mold of what he thinks I want, and then realize that it is just not "him". I guess in my dreams I would like a partner who will be beside me and I beside him for life...that he would delight in the essence of me and cherish me.

My man would love the simple things in life, like walking hand in hand, enjoying a home cooked meal, looking at the

stars, and engaging in deep conversation.
He would be able to communicate his feelings in a spirit of openness and trust, knowing that all his secrets are safe with me, and that I would never knowingly do or say anything to hurt him. To be able to look into his eyes and be completely content, knowing that this was ordained by God.
I think that the most important thing for me is that I could be myself in a relationship...to not feel that I have to 'perform' to be loved;

Describe a little of your personality and character traits. (Are you funny, laid back, more serious, open, shy, etc.?)

I am generally laid back, a little on the timid side. I have a good sense of humor, sometimes dry. I think that my best quality is that I am an eternal optimist.... my glass is always half full, and I tend to see the best in people, even when others don't. I believe in second chances.
I have a lot of friends and a lot of long-time friends. I don't take friendships lightly, and each person who is my friend today knows that I am a true, loyal and loving one. I am gracious, modest, diplomatic, and affectionate...I usually do well in any situation and with many different types of people.

What are your favorite activities? (Including sports, leisure, artistic/musical, etc.)

I love to read, watch movies, read, ride bike, eat out, and did I mention that I like to read? Going for a drive or a walk in the mountains is always a big hit with me. I enjoy shopping in different places and bargain hunting. I am always drawn to open-air markets, as they seem to have a laid-back summertime atmosphere.

I also very much enjoy hands on activities, like cooking, crafts, and gardening.

I am a morning coffee type of person. Along with my coffee I like to tackle the crossword and Sudoku puzzles of the day...sometimes I actually solve them.

How did your previous relationship end and what positive lessons have you learned which will help you succeed in future relationships?

Adultery.

I have learned that if it walks like a duck, talks like a duck and looks like a duck, it must be a duck...you should believe it.

Throughout my time on the Christian Café, which was a few years, I met a lot of interesting characters, men as well as women.

Before long I was on a few dating sites: Lavalife, Christian Café, Seniors Meet, Plenty of Fish and E Harmony, to name a few. I met lots of people, but like me, they were mostly deficient in some way and emotionally unsuitable. At one point a friend said I should write a book about my experiences and call it <u>Idiots I Have Known</u>. I never did do that but I'll tell about some of them here so you can see the futility of dating sites and long-distance dating. I've changed all the names (in the rare instance that one of them ends up reading this)

First there was Paul from Virginia. He told me at the outset that he had big financial troubles. I really liked him, but his finances were what finished us in the end.

Harry, another American, never took anything seriously. He just wanted to instant message, and after calling me once, he disappeared.

Mike was a trucker from a cold western state. My first impression was that he was emotionally unbalanced. As I got to know him better, my suspicions were confirmed.

Leroy was a nice guy but still in school, poor, and not ready for a relationship. I don't know what he was doing on a dating site.

Jake was a bit of a scammer in that he kept signing up for the site under different aliases so he wouldn't have to pay for a membership. He sent me songs and stories and talked about sex a lot.

My first impression of Daniel was that he was a player with lots of women on a string. It turned out to be true, but I only found out after he broke my heart.

Richard was totally inappropriate. All he could talk about was slave and master, dominant women and how much he liked legs and feet.

Keith lied about his age, and he talked so much it was like verbal diarrhea. I contemplated picking my nose to get his attention.

Henry jumped me on the second date and said that it wouldn't be casual sex. This from a man who had been married only long enough to impregnate his wife and then she left. I wondered why.

Dave was from Vermont and extremely jealous. He assumed too much too soon about our nonexistent relationship. He sent me a lot of hate mail once he realized I wasn't interested.

Joe was married and divorced three times and he broke an engagement for the fourth one. Need I say more?

Tim was a private investigator from Arkansas and turned out to be an angry, controlling pervert. He called once at 2 AM to talk about sex.

Men who lived within driving distance were able to come to my town and I met each of them at a restaurant, interestingly called Scores. I had my booth there where we shared a coffee and got to know each other. But most of the time I was Treacle from 'une petite ville Francais and I could hide behind that name in the chat rooms and dating sites because I was still very much broken.

24

Letters to Jamie on the Christian Cafe

Basically, the men I met online were a bust, but there were some women who became friends and we corresponded for a time, comparing notes, and commiserating with each other. One day a woman from Texas contacted me to see how I was doing on the site and so we began a long correspondence, cheering each other on. I saved some of our letters because they make me laugh, even now.

October 14

Hey Chrissie: I love hearing from you. I have no love life. I went on a date with the Mike from Huntsville. It was horrible. He looked at the little Texas A & M girls all night and would state, "I don't know how my son controls himself around here". He also ordered for us, I had no say so, and he told the waitress that we would share something. Then, we came right back to my house, when he had said that we would go to a movie. He then wanted to know if I would sleep with him and I said "no", so he left. He was gone by 9:00, which was fine with me. Creep! A complete waste of my time. Hope your life is better.

October 14
Hi Jamie,

How have you been doing? And how are things with Mike? I have missed our exchanges!

Have been having busy weeks with teaching and family in from out of town, and today I am bringing my parents to Ottawa (two hours away) and back. So, it has been life in the fast lane.

I have met (online) two men on here. We are corresponding, and they both seem nice, one from Ontario and the other from the States. I am so afraid of rejection sometimes that I think they are all going to disappear.... oh well, part of my baggage!!

Love to hear from you when you have time.
Chrissie

October 18
Hi Chrissie

      Hope you have done better than me. I went out with the Huntsville Mike again. He called me every night for three weeks. Then, on our last date, he wanted to go to bed, but I never really liked him like that. I had told him that I wouldn't sleep with him unless we had some kind of commitment. He went to the door and told me it was probably the last time I would see him. I said 'fine' and then he left. Men are so weird. Can you believe that he called me three weeks straight, let me meet his son, and then dumped me. He said it was really hard for him to commit. He also lied about his age on his profile. He is

57 years old but looks older and walks like an old guy. He just isn't that appealing to go to bed with.

October 20
Hi Jamie,
      I have been corresponding daily, sometimes for hours, with a Mike from Ontario. He wants to come and meet me in person next month. We'll see.

To tell you the truth, I am scared to death. My ex was so into sex I never felt like a person. He demanded it all the time and said that I had to submit to him. Now after talking to numerous people including my pastor, they have made me understand that I was sexually abused by my ex. So, I go into a new relationship with fear and trepidation, I can tell you.

October 22
Hi Jamie,
      Well, here I sit, again. Yesterday Mike told me that he has someone waiting for him in Texas. Sounds like he was trying to choose between us. I must really be a lunatic magnet. I'm about to throw in the towel on all this. It's disheartening, to say the least. I get my emotions involved every time. Feeling down right now.
      Chrissie

October 22
Hey Chrissie,

I do know what you mean. I met this other guy, and we were just going to a movie and then for something to eat. For the first time since my divorce, here was someone I liked.

I can't believe that the last guy contacted me again and told me I was playing games with him. I wasn't the one who did the ditching--he did. He's a creep and a pervert. I didn't tell you, but the whole time I was out with him, he looked at little college girls and made dirty remarks. Finally, I told him that it made me uncomfortable. He asked me if I thought he could get a young girl. I said yes you can if you have money. Then he said, "Can I get one that speaks in tongues?" I was mortified.

October 30
Hi Jamie,

There's nothing new here, and that might be a good thing. My sister is getting so frustrated with me because she sees me getting emotionally involved with all these lunatics online. She thinks I should meet people from around here instead. The only problem is that I need someone around my age, Christian and English.

That's a tall order for here, as Quebec is predominantly French, a mission field and full of men with accents who want to jump in bed before even meeting. I am seriously contemplating moving from here to an English place, but it would wreck my family. But then again, if I'm not happy, what's the use? I have

to go get my son up for school. You have a great day! Write me back- you're a ray of sunshine on here for me.
Chrissie

October 31
Hi Chrissie
I just told my daughter that it's worth it to be on here because I get to talk to you. What would I do without you? I just got ditched by a guy named Randall and I really liked him, not that it made any difference. I just don't understand why these guys don't like me. I'm so tired of this.
Jamie

November 2
Hi Jamie,
      It does get tiring, doesn't it? I just had to tell someone on here for the umpteenth time today that I don't want a relationship with him, but just to be friends. He's an emotional basket case. You and I need to get into our heads that we are nice people, probably some of the sanest on here. I have met so many nut cases I wonder where all the good men are.
  I'm getting ready to sell my Divorce Fudge for Christmas for the second year in a row. Hopefully it will be the success it was last year. Write me back.
Chrissie

November 16
Hi Chrissie

I just can't not tell you about this last one. I went to Denny's to meet him because I knew it was safe. He weighed 450 lbs. He had no teeth. He had a truck filled, and I mean filled, with trash. He asked me to marry him as soon as I drove up. Oh yeah, did I mention that he said he contracted something in Vietnam and he has a problem with sweating and can't control it. This is absolutely the truth if I ever told it. Do you think God is trying to tell me something?

Then yesterday afternoon I had an email from another man who wanted me to go to a motorcycle rally with him. I went and had a really great time, and he works for the government. I love motorcycles and have one myself. He was so nice and he told me that he was going to ask me to marry him on Tuesday, but had to knock his teeth out and gain some weight first. Cool sense of humor. Write me.

Jamie November 17
Aw Jamie,

I'm laughing my head off as I write this. Did you meet this sweating ape on this site?

November 19
Hi Chrissie

At least I made you laugh. It was all the truth too. Yes, I met him on here and I was so surprised. He said that he had a few extra pounds, and he did; about 300 of them. He was

so obese that he had to walk with a cane. I got angry. When I came home and told my daughter, she started laughing and then finally I laughed as well and that made me feel better. But I was mean to this man, and I have never been mean to anyone. Everything he said was a lie. Like you're not going to be able to see with your own eyes that they're lying. I have to go to work. I work in a prison with liars, thieves and perverts, so why am I surprised? I look forward to hearing from you.
Jamie

The last time I heard from Jamie, she was going to marry a man that she had gone out with once. She said she figured she didn't have a lot of time left and no one was going to change her mind. I hope she fared out ok.

During all this time I was still very much under the influence of the cult, although I had started wearing pants sometimes. Wearing them made me feel guilty, as if I was committing a sin. And then I thought about my husband, with another woman. That was a sin too. My thought patterns were the same as before and that's why I looked for a 'take charge' man, one who would take care of me and fulfill all my needs. I had no idea what a real and normal married life would look like; the only way I knew how to be in a relationship was my first marriage. The man was supposed to lead, and the woman was supposed to submit and respond to the leading. The man was supposed to provide for his family and the woman was to be a keeper at home. This is Patriarchy, pure and simple. I knew that but didn't realize that patriarchy is not a good thing, especially for me. I needed to grow some balls, get a backbone, and decide for myself how I wanted to live.

I had no idea how I wanted to live because for so many years I had lived by biblical principles and rules and regulations. In ATI, we had been taught that if you 'follow these seven steps' or 'develop all these character qualities' you would have a happy and successful life. Well, that didn't happen in my marriage. Where did I go wrong?

I visited my old pastor Marius a few times at Lakeshore Church in Dorval, to tell him the details of what had happened to my marriage and to have some support. We had attended this church for several years before we became too holy for an organized church. But now I was back, and Marius welcomed me with open arms. Sitting in his office and discussing my plight in life and my options felt like being home. I was comfortable with him because he really knew what I was talking about. He and his wife had visited our home in addition to knowing us from church. Remember, it was Marius and his wife that noticed I kept looking to my husband for approval anytime I spoke.

I still think of the day we were drinking coffee in his office, and I was complaining and lamenting. Marius told me that my ex wasn't happy. How could he be happy?

I said to Marius, "Well, from my vantage point he's doing pretty darn good. He has a new partner, he travels, he buys whatever he wants. How can you say he isn't happy?"

And then Marius explained to me that those were all superficial things, and that when my ex would look at himself in the mirror (and he had to do that every day to shave), he would not like the person he had become. He would be tortured about how he had destroyed his family. It would make him miserable. It took me a lot of years before I began to believe what Marius was saying.

As the saying goes, 'What goes around comes around'. After sixteen years together, my ex and his partner have split up. I find it strange that I take no satisfaction in hearing this. I feel sad for both of them. I guess Marius was right.

25

First Soulful, Romantic Encounter

And then there was Don.
We met on the Christian Café in the Spring of 2005, just eight months after my marriage breakup. Don was a struggling lawyer in North Carolina trying to raise three kids, and I was a struggling ex-cult member in Quebec, also with three kids.

Unaware of Southern charm, and craving validation, I was swept off my feet with Don's online attention. He told me I was gorgeous. He told me I was smart, and he listened to me. That's how Southerners are; I believed every word and I'm sure he was sincere.

Over a period of two months, we fell in love over the phone and online. He wrote me poetry. We read books together and discussed them. He introduced me to varieties of music, as I had only listened to hymns and classical pieces for the previous years in the religious cult that ruled my life. It felt as if we were soul mates and intellectual equals. There wasn't anything sexier than that for me. I could see into his heart, and he could see into mine.

With the Montreal Jazz Fest looming, I asked Don if he would like to come up to take in a few concerts. I was not familiar with jazz, but I knew he loved it.

He said yes! And then he bought tickets to a couple of concerts and booked his flight. He also booked a hotel in the heart of Montreal, on Crescent St, the Hotel Royale. Then he went on a diet so that he could present his best self to me.

On the day Don arrived, I was all set with a new dress, sky blue with scattered flowers, red sandals to match, a fresh haircut and a smile that held the promise of new love. The enormous zit that had sprouted under my nose was well taken care of with thick makeup. My son drove me to the airport way too early, and so I found a place to sit and wait for Don.

My cell phone rang.

It was Don, wondering where he was supposed to go now that he was off the plane. He was joking, but just wanted to hear my voice and to tease me. As my excitement mounted and my innards turned to mush, I talked him through the corridors, the revolving doors, the moving walkway and the crowds until we stood face to face.

Every fiber of my body was tingling; even fibers I thought had died with menopause and age.

Don held me at arm's length and said, "You're even prettier in person!" Gazing into each other's eyes we could see the innermost essence of each other's being. I have never, not before and not since that moment, felt such a deep connection with another human being.

The poems, music, conversations and understanding all melted into that one moment, the moment we met in person for the first time. There were people rushing to and fro in the Montreal airport that day. There were officials, taxi drivers, important people, rich people, all manner of noise and confusion, but in that moment, there was only Don and I having our first kiss, so private in such a public place. Everything else melted away as we clung to each other, hearts pounding and falling more in love than I ever thought possible.

I felt young, beautiful, and desirable again.

26

The Day My Heart Broke

Liminal space was a good description of how the bottom had come out of my world and everything became new to me again.

The five years between my two marriages was a free-falling, liminal time. Don came along and scooped me up from my terrified position, calmed my fears, and made me feel beautiful and loved.

After our first meeting in the airport in 2005, we began a three-year on-again, off-again relationship.

In 2005 Don told me he loved me but that he had nothing to offer me. He was a struggling lawyer in North Carolina with three kids and a lot of debt. He said he couldn't subject my son and I to that.

But we were in love.

Things at home in Quebec were becoming intolerable for me, with my ex constantly harassing me to go to work and support the children and myself. That would have been difficult because I had been out of the workforce for 21 years, during which time I had homeschooled my children within the confines of ATI. My divorce left me afraid of everything outside my kitchen window, and the harassment was depressing me further.

I decided to take my youngest son out of his new school and take him to Myrtle Beach, South Carolina for two months, to get away from my ex and to be closer to Don.

We fell more in love, but Don had debt coming out his ears and incurring more every day. In my mind he wasn't great at managing his finances. When I returned to Quebec at the end of the two months, I had a feeling we were saying goodbye, and I was sad.

Sure enough, by Summer of 2006 Don had broken it off with me, saying that his finances were getting worse, that he was on a downward spiral, and that he didn't know who or how he would be at the end of it.

We both cried.

There was no contact for the next year and a half. During that time, I went on many dating sites, looking for Mr. Right. I met lots of men, but I imagined every one of them was Don. I was still heartbroken. I continued to meet them at Scores Restaurant in St. Eustache, but it was futile because during our conversation and coffee, I imagined it was Don sitting there and not this stranger.

Finally, one Christmas Day I was sitting in bed with my computer and still thinking of Don. I decided to be brave and write him, just to say hello and that I hoped he was happy. I told him about my kids and my life, never really expecting to hear from him again.

He wrote me back! He sent me photos of himself and his children, and he updated me on his life. And then…and then he said he wanted to see me, that he had something to tell me.

He sent me a plane ticket to fly down to North Carolina and spend a few days with him. This time we met at another airport, in Raleigh NC, but now we fell into each other's arms, shed a few tears, laughed, cried some more, hugged, gazed into each other's eyes, and then we went for a meal.

After all, it was Valentine's Day. Don gave me flowers and over supper he told me that he'd never stopped loving me, that his financial situation had changed, that he wanted to raise my son as his own and that he wanted to marry me. We were both so very happy.

Over the next several months we opened a request for a fiancée visa, I put my house on the market, I sold my car and prepared to leave Canada with my youngest son. But even though there were plenty of prospective buyers for my house, not one of them made an offer. I wondered why my friend's house, three doors down and identical to mine, had only a couple of visits and sold immediately. My house had even more features than hers, and my basement was finished, driveway paved. Hers wasn't. As I checked off the items on the visa list and our move to North Carolina became imminent, I fretted and worried about the house. I couldn't leave Canada with my house unsold, could I?

And then I remembered what my friend Michelle had said a few years earlier about moving to Newfoundland and I paraphrased her words to my present situation.

"If your house is not selling now, it's because it's not the right time for it to sell. When it's the right time it will be easy."

Well, this wasn't easy at all. When would be the right time if not now? I wondered what forces beyond my control were at work. Should I just wait? What was the rush? During this time, Don had a business deal fall through, the housing market in the States was plummeting, and once again finances threatened to destroy our happiness. He said that he 'still' wanted to marry me but that I was boarding a sinking ship. He became passive-aggressive. I became depressed.

    I went down to North Carolina for a month that summer and saw things begin to crack. My Southern Gentleman showed me another side of himself. A not so pretty side. He had become mean, borderline nasty and snapped at me over the slightest provocation. He wasn't as romantic as he had claimed to be. I knew it was because of his financial tension but did he have to take it out on me? He said he was stressed once again over his finances, but I didn't think that was a good excuse to be impatient with me and I told him so. I found myself shrinking away from him. I still didn't think I had the right to feel safe in a relationship, that I had to go along with whatever came my way. My cult mentality of submission kept me from really speaking my mind.

    I went back to Quebec with many questions, doubts, and dark thoughts. I wrestled with my situation for the next two months: Could I, in all good faith, go to live in the United States? Could I bring my adolescent son to a small North Carolina town with guns and racial tensions? He didn't want to leave his school, his brothers, his friends, his town, nor his country. I started to have a pain in my gut that wouldn't go away. At the eleventh hour I broke up with my Southern gentleman. I took my house off the market. I bought another car. I wrote a letter to the American Embassy explaining why I was putting a halt to the visa process. All my papers were in order and at that point I was just waiting for the letter inviting me to the Embassy for my interview and to have my passport stamped. After this happened, I would have a specified number of days to leave Canada and move to the United States. My letter crossed paths with the embassy's letter in the mail because three days after sending mine, I received their approval of my application and the invitation.

  I think the saddest day of my life was the day I broke it off with Don for the last time, just three days before my Visa came through. I became quite depressed and ended up on medication. I really needed some help in understanding what I had done and more than that, I needed some self-validation. My confidence was still in the gutter. I called my old pastor, Marius, and we agreed to meet at a coffee shop halfway between where we both lived.

  Marius could see my sadness and uncertainty and so we hashed the situation out together. We made a list of my reasons for breaking it off with Don and discussed each one. Marius was able to make me see that I was worth more than I had previously thought. He pointed out all my strong traits that I was unable to see at the time. He thought I was engaging, funny, I expressed myself very well, and that I had a lot to offer. Even if I had been able to see my strengths, I had been trained to defer and deflect, never to claim ownership of who I really was.

At the end of our conversation, I realized that I had made the right decision, even if it made me sad. I think that half of my sadness was that I would never have a chance at happiness, that it was for other people, but not for me. I couldn't imagine anyone loving me for who I was, warts, hang-ups, baggage, and all.

Over a long period of time, I came to be at peace with my memories of that phase of my life, when I was in liminal space and Don was there to show me that life wasn't so terrifying. Sometimes now I think of him, but more with bittersweet thoughts.

27

Depressed- Who, Me?

However, in the interim, I became quite depressed, but didn't recognize it as such. I was so used to denying my feelings and desires that my breakup with Don just felt like another disappointment and that happiness was for others, but not for me. I pasted on my smile like I had always done and went about my life.

About a month after the breakup, there was a St Francis Xavier University get-together for the Montreal alumni chapter. It was at my favourite restaurant, le Biftheque, a wonderful steakhouse. My sister was going with a friend and asked me if I'd join them. I said yes, but really didn't want to go. But I did go because I wanted to be brave. It was a long drive in the dark from my little house in Deux Montagnes, all the way to St Laurent Boulevard on the West Island of Montreal that November evening. I had put on my best clothes that fit and began the drive down highway 13. I cried all the way. Arriving at le Biftheque, I wiped my tears, blew my nose and pasted on my smile. We had a great time, and the food was outstanding, as usual. When it was all over, I got in my car and cried all the way up highway 13 and finally was able to go to bed with my dark thoughts.

I awakened to the ringing of the phone beside my bed. It was my sister, very concerned about me. She said she thought I was depressed. I told her that I did my best to smile and be my jovial self at the restaurant last evening. And that's when she said that no one but she would have been able to notice that even though I was smiling, my eyes were dead. Because she knew me so well, she could see through my fragile veneer what others could not. I broke down on the phone with her and admitted that I was in utter despair, sadness, and loneliness. She helped me to understand that I needed to see my doctor for some help. But it would take months to get an appointment.

I felt so desperate, that as soon as my doctor's office opened, I just showed up and spoke to Manon, the receptionist. She knew me and could see that something was seriously wrong. I was so grateful that she squeezed me in to see Dr. Bovo, my longtime doctor, almost immediately. Dr. Bovo could see that I was in distress and so she gave me the questionnaire they give to possibly depressed people. I passed with flying colours- I was definitely depressed and needed some help right now.

I felt ashamed for needing anti-depressants. Wasn't I supposed to be strong enough to overcome this? I had been taught that melodious music, a tidy house and lots of prayer could combat depression. Only weak people need pills, or so I thought.

I started to take them despite my negative feelings about needing a crutch, and in about two weeks they kicked in beautifully. It was as if I was seeing the world through a different pair of glasses. I slept better, I felt better, I was more pleasant, I cried less, and the feelings of despair faded away. I finally had the time to have the breakdown I was on the brink of for many years. I could finally admit to my weakness and my need for understanding and compassion. At that point I was angry that I had endured several years of misery because I was too proud to admit weakness and take the darn pills. Those pills saved my life, I think. I was ashamed of thinking that melodious music, prayer and a tidy house would pull me out of the pit.

28

Single Again

Here I was, single again with no man or marriage in sight. As the months passed, I found myself more and more dependent on the idea of having a man to take care of me. In ATI, women were discouraged from being independent. They were to submit to their husbands. This mindset was still very much with me. But without a husband I felt that I had no direction for my life, and no purpose. And all the men I had met online and then in person were deficient in some way, just like me.

I decided that I probably wasn't ready for another relationship. I realized that the only person who could save me was me, myself. I couldn't rely on a partner to pull me out of the mire and take care of me. I needed to prove to myself and the world that I was capable of taking care of myself. And I might as well accept that it would probably take some work on my part. There was a lot of work in healing from my divorce and learning to love myself. That was a difficult task because in ATI we were taught to die to self and serve others. I was still very much under the cult teachings, so this learning to love myself came with some guilt. Imagine feeling guilty for taking care of yourself!

As time went on, so did my miserable life, until one day I realized that I was doing this all wrong. I could see that I wasn't such a great catch with all the baggage I was still carrying. Before I could be a fit partner for anyone, I had to do two things. First, I had to take my ex to court once and for all in order to be financially free of him. This was incredibly difficult for me because I still saw him as an authority figure in my life, even though we had now been divorced for four years.

The final straw was when my sister went to the bank with me to cash a child support check. He had put a stop payment on it. I had sunk to a new and humiliating low. My sister ended up buying my groceries that day, much to my shame. But, as she explained, it was not shameful for me; it was shameful for my ex to not support his family.

That was all I needed to send me back to my lawyer. We discussed getting a settlement from my ex that would free me from him forever. The plan was to send a bailiff to his door with a subpoena to appear in court in a few weeks. But at that point he didn't have a door for the bailiff to go to. He was staying somewhere in the Laurentians at his new partner's daughter's place, and I thought I knew where he was. My back-door friend, Wanda, was going through her own divorce at that time, and we visited often and commiserated. It seemed that whenever I was doing good, she wasn't, and when she was doing well, I wasn't. So, we were able to support each other.

I went to see Wanda and asked her to call that place in the Laurentians and ask for my ex by name. We sat in her living room, hearts pounding and laughing nervously while she blocked herself by dialing *67 and dialed the number. That way the call display would say 'unknown'. A woman answered and Wanda asked for my ex. If he came to the phone, then we knew where to send the bailiff and she would hang up. He answered, but when his hello was met with silence, he asked Wanda what she was doing. Darn. The call blocking, for some strange reason, had not worked, and he saw her name and number on the call display. But now we knew for sure where he was. And he knew who was looking for him.

Wanda and I laughed hysterically for some time after that. But it was more nervousness than mirth.

I called my lawyer the next day and told her where he was. The wheels were set in motion. The bailiff made his way to the Laurentians and presented my ex with the subpoena. I could only imagine his shock because I don't think he ever considered that I would make such a move.

On the eve of our court date, my son was performing at a concert in Montreal. Many of my friends and family came in support of my son and also of me. My parents were there as well. We were all standing in the lobby waiting for the concert hall to open and I was pretty much hiding behind my sister as my ex walked in, alone. I was still afraid of him and how he might bawl me out for the subpoena and court date the next morning. When the concert was over, my dad, learning about the suppressed drama and tension that had preceded the concert, said something to me that I've never forgotten.

"Christine, you're going to have to learn to assert yourself!"

That was the day I realized that I had nothing to fear except my own irrational thoughts and that I had rights. When in a situation with other people that feels uncomfortable, my father's words still ring in my ears. I'm asserting myself more and more every day.

Early the next morning, I drove up Highway 15 to the Palais de Justice in St. Jerome, with Wanda at my side. We made it as far as the courthouse on that Friday morning, but never got in front of the judge because we settled 'in the hallway'. Wanda and I were in one little room with my lawyer, Brigette, and Ex and his partner were in another little room with his lawyer. The lawyers discussed in the hallway and went to their respective rooms to report. That day I left the courthouse with two checks and some freedom. There was one for alimony and another for child support. Wanda and I went out for a nice lunch at St Hubert BBQ and rehashed everything together.

My life instantly became lighter and more hopeful. It wasn't easy for me to move on while I was still tied to someone who had a spiritual, financial, and emotional hold on me, even if that hold was only in my mind. A belief system is a very powerful thing.

The next thing I had to do to become a person fit to have a relationship with someone else and to be a part of society, was to get a job, any job, so that I could support myself. I couldn't decide to marry someone just so that I could live off them. I needed to know that I could take care of myself. Then I could decide whether or not I wanted another relationship. The problem was that I only knew how to teach; that's all I had done my whole adult life. I needed something different because I was quite tired of teaching children, including my own.

I heard of a course being offered by the government of Quebec for people over 50 who were in transition in their lives. I went to the Centre d'Emploi du Quebec in St Eustache, where a lady named Carole got me signed up for this course. It was 9 to 5, five days a week, just like a real job. There were about eighteen of us in the course and most of them, like me, had some sad story that brought them there, whether it was through being laid off from their job or getting back in the workforce after a long absence. We got to know each other pretty well and did a lot of soul searching during the twelve weeks of the course. We learned how to look for a job, how to find something in our line of interest, how to tailor a resume to the job, and we finished up with doing mockup interviews on video.

That's how I ended up working at a lavender farm, just outside St. Eustache. They were looking for 'mature' women to work at their new farm, in the boutique. I was 'mature' and I loved lavender. In my cover letter I included a sprig of lavender from my own plant at home. They must have been impressed because I was hired on the spot.

29
Lavender Saved Me

During the last seven months I lived in Quebec, I worked at a lavender farm. Finally, this teacher could put the schoolbooks on the shelf and go to work at Pure Lavande, now known as La Maison Lavande, owned by Nancie Ferron and Daniel Joannette, just on the outskirts of St Eustache. I have to say those were the most rewarding and hectic months imaginable.

The learning curve was huge. I learned many of the benefits of lavender and taught them to the visitors. I told them, "Lavender is antiseptic, anti-spasmodic, antibacterial, repels mice and mosquitoes, and is very easy to grow".

The farm boasted about 70,000 lavender plants in a field behind the boutique. On approaching the site, visitors were treated to the delightful and calming scent of lavender. Some would stand in the doorway of the boutique and just exclaim, "Ahhh, lavender!" They would always leave with at least one of the thirty-five products on display, or they would decide to buy a lavender plant to have their own piece of heaven at home.

Lavender is so easy to grow; it thrives in nutrient-poor soil, repels most insects, and requires very little water. In fact, we used to tell the customers to plant the lavender in a sunny spot in well-drained soil and to refrain from watering it, as lavender roots don't like to sit in moisture.

I'll never forget the lady who bought a plant one Sunday and was given all the instructions for care and planting.

On Monday she was back in the boutique very agitated. She earnestly explained that she was told not to water the lavender, but now they were forecasting rain, and she was afraid to lose her lovely plant.

I was the resident Anglaise, the only person on the premises who could speak English, so I was called upon regularly to serve the English customers who came from as far away as Alberta, and to translate for the many journalists who wanted to interview Nancie and Daniel for their English publications. I'll never forget the day one posh magazine editor from Toronto arrived for her interview in a brand-new flaming red Mercedes. The lavender was in full bloom and so they took pictures of the red Mercedes surrounded by an ocean of lavender. Absolutely stunning!

I loved my job and was happy there at the farm. It was such a positive place to be, no one ever came there in a bad mood and for the first time in years I felt like I belonged. We had lots of laughs as well. One day a woman came into the boutique and wanted to sample some of the products. I showed her the soap and sachets, had her try the lavender room spray and then she picked up another product that was vanilla and lavender. Spraying it all over herself, she delighted in the scent and the experience until I told her that was a spray for pets, to repel fleas. We both had a great laugh that day.

Another time, a couple came into the boutique and as they made their way around, looking at all the products, I noticed them looking strangely at me. Finally, they approached and engaged me in conversation. And when they were just about sure, they asked me if I used to be married to a Chiropractor. They had been patients at the clinic a few years prior, and seeing me now, they couldn't believe I was the same person. They told me I was cute, vivacious, and welcoming. That was a huge compliment because I was none of those things during my marriage.

The scent of lavender is very calming, and that is just what I needed at that point in my life. I spent my days serving customers, wrapping lavender bouquets, filling sachets, and cutting and wrapping soap. I also sold my Divorce Fudge at the boutique, but it was called 'Sucre a la Crème a la Lavande' and was sprinkled with edible lavender. I had so much fun there and made new friends. I was surprised to see that everyone at the farm loved not only my accent, but they also loved me. I, who had felt so unlovable, was now being praised by her new employers and leading groups around the boutique to tell them all about the products.

My job gave me not only the confidence that I was so lacking but also the finances to be able to live life on my terms. I felt free and happy for the first time in many years. I had fulfilled the two criteria to make myself into a woman with the grace to be a fit partner for whomever might come along, or to be my own self in the world as a single person. Either way, I knew I was going to make it.

30

I Had Forgotten Who I Was

For most of the years I was married and in the confines of ATI, I shut myself off from people I had known and loved for most of my life. We were just too different. How could I explain my unique lifestyle to my old university buddies? They would never understand all the things we did and didn't do. At first some of them used to call, but as we got further and further into Biblical Principles, the phone calls first became strained and uncomfortable, and then they stopped altogether. I didn't really mind at the time because we were on a different path, a Godly path, and we thought we were better than everyone else, including my old university friends.

It was alienating when family came to visit. One time when my sister was visiting, she in her favourite jeans and a t-shirt, me in the requisite jumper with a modest blouse underneath, we were having a conversation. In exasperation she told me how our lifestyle made her feel.

"You and your family are like a wheel- God is at the center and all the spokes emanating from the center represent the different parts of your life, like movies, how you dress, how you eat, how you live. For me, I am at the center of the wheel and the spokes represent the other facets of my life. God is simply one of the spokes."

It was true. But I didn't take her comment as the criticism that it was. I was happy she noticed that God was at the center of my life. In my pride I failed to see her point. I could only see mine because my blinders were very effective.

Sometime after my divorce, and old friend found me on Facebook, and we started communicating. Jenny had been my closest friend all through university and beyond. We had lived on the same floor in residence at St Francis Xavier University in Antigonish, NS, and then we shared an apartment for another year. We did a lot of silly things together. She knew that I had 'gone right religious' before my divorce but now she wanted to see me again. Jenny flew to Montreal and came to stay at my little house for a few days. My son remembers those days "as the time that lady came and all you two did was laugh while sitting on your respective couches."

It was true. We had a lot of laughs and a lot of reminiscences. It troubled me that there were some things she brought up that I couldn't remember. At all. A lot of our conversation during that visit started with, "Remember when we…" but I didn't remember. She kept trying to remind me of where we had been and what we were doing but, try as I might, I was not able to bring those things to memory. I must have blocked out certain incidents from my consciousness because they were so incongruent with the lifestyle I subsequently led.

Jenny was the friend who looked as if she had been crying at my wedding all those years ago. Now she could tell me about it. Apparently, at the wedding reception at my parents' house, my new husband, knowing of mine and Jenny's friendship, said to her, "Christine won't be needing you anymore because now she has me." And I had wondered all those years what had become of Jenny. So many lost years.

I think of another friend, Bill, who ended up in Alberta at the same time as me. I spent some time with him and his wife Eve, even though they lived in Edmonton, and I was two hours north in High Prairie. Bill still reminds me of the Halloween that Eve and I dressed up as women of the night and he dressed up as our pimp. Apparently, we had gotten on a city bus with an extra-large pizza that took up too much space in the crowded bus. We were heading to a party, and we were laughing our heads off. People on the bus were just a little startled to see the lot of us. Bill still laughs when telling that story. To this day I have no recollection of that time. But I do remember the time he called me at 3AM to tell me that he had just called the Pope and had gotten right to the Vatican before he was cut off.

   I guess the mind is an amazing thing; it can recall things that can help us but also can block out things that our present self would not be willing to acknowledge. It makes me sad sometimes that those things have been erased from my mind, and I wonder about all the other things that I must have forgotten.

31

How I Met My New Husband

These days I am living in rural Nova Scotia with my second husband. We live on a crescent in a little town in an area where there are neither sidewalks nor streetlamps. When we go for a walk in the evening, we have to bring a flashlight. And I am living the life I have always wanted to live. When my old life crashed and burned, I didn't know that this life was waiting for me. But it was.

Back in 1973 when I was a student at St Francis Xavier University, I had a little job a few hours a week at the information booth of the Student Union Building. My job was to answer the phone and give out keys and information, also to man the lost and found drawer. It was there that I met a young man who would become one of my best friends and thirty-six years later, my husband. Since I was the dispenser of information, he asked me, "How many legs are there on a snake?" And a friendship started. It's funny, but back then we never dated or were romantic. We were just friends, and we stayed that way for the duration of my time at St FX until I graduated in 1975.   In the summer of 1975, Dave was on his way to Lewisporte, Newfoundland to get married, and he had to pass through Corner Brook, where I was home for the summer with my family. He stayed at my parents' place for a couple of days, and I showed him the sights of the West Coast of Newfoundland. He met all my family, and my mom just loved him because of his lighthearted spirit and his ability to make me laugh. And then he left Corner Brook and got married. We went our separate ways; he ended up living in Nova Scotia and had three children and I ended up married with three children and living in Quebec. We had no contact for many years. On a random day in March 1994, my husband came to see me with a puzzled look on his face.

He said, "There's a man on the phone who wants to talk to you. He said his name is Dave Jones." A flood of memories came back to me in that instant, of my days back in university when Dave was one of my best friends. We chatted a bit, but we each were still entangled in our respective lives. To tell the truth, I had just, two weeks before, given birth to my third son. With my cult mindset and answering to my husband in everything, I was nervous talking to this voice from my past. Why was he calling me? I was happily married; at least that's the story everyone, including me, believed. He followed up with a long newsy letter and at the time, being that my life was so busy with a nursing baby, homeschooling and a demanding husband that I told him I wasn't able to communicate with him. In the cult the belief was that a woman should not have any kind of friendship with another man.

Ten years later, in 2004, my marriage was over, and I moved to a new house with the children. I had all but forgotten my friends from St FX, and so much time had passed that it had never occurred to me to contact any of them. Besides, I figured that after such a long absence of contact, none of them would be interested in hearing from me. Some of them knew that I had "gone right religious" so our lives were literally and geographically miles apart. Living in a French town and not working made it virtually impossible to have a social life. I lived in my little house, substitute taught at a school nearby, and took care of my kids. And then in 2005 I started the internet dating. I was on every site I could find. In addition to Christian Café, I joined Lavalife, Lavalife Prime, Plenty of Fish, Christian Mingle and others. Sometimes I would have three chat rooms and instant messaging going on all at the same time. It was fun, but at the end of the day I was still alone in my little cookie cutter house in Deux Montagnes, and all of my new friends were just virtual friends.

In 2007 I heard of Facebook. My son told me that you had to be a university student to get on Facebook. I believed him until one of my friends told me that she was a member. I immediately put up a profile and started adding friends. Imagine my delight when I started getting friend requests from people that I hadn't heard from in years. People from my hometown, Corner Brook, NL; people I had worked with; old university buddies: Jenny, Rosie, Raylene, Eve, Bill, Anna, and others. And then in 2008 I received a friend request from my old friend Dave. We exchanged a couple of emails just updating each other on our respective lives. We laughed to hear that we each had had three children and a divorce! But at that time, we were both entangled in other relationships, so a few emails were all the contact we had. In the meantime, another friend who lived not far from Dave in the Annapolis Valley, started talking to me about him; I kept trying to tell her that Dave was in a relationship and so was I, but she just kept on. Little did I know that she was also talking to Dave about me!

On a cold February day that year, I had posted on Facebook that my car needed repairs. I can't remember what the problem was or why I posted that. I guess I was sitting at home, bored because there had been a snowstorm, the schools were closed, and I had lost a day of substitute teaching. I received an email from Dave asking me about my car and also telling me that in Nova Scotia there had been a snowstorm, so he had the day off.

Hmmm… We exchanged a few emails in quick succession, and then I wrote him, "Why don't you just call: 450 473 2629. A couple of minutes later the phone rang and Dave and I had a conversation for the first time since 1994. The years melted away as we got caught up on each other's lives, and we laughed and joked as if we had seen each other just the other day. Before I knew it, we were saying goodbye and an hour and a half had passed. When we hung up, I was still smiling at the connection we had just made, but I was sad as I thought of what might have been. We were both still in relationships and there would be nothing between us.

That spring I got an email from Dave telling me that he was going to Calgary to visit his son for a few days. He asked me if I would be free for a coffee if he had a stopover in Montreal on the way. I told him I would be free indeed and would love to meet with him. And so, the date was set for July 23, 2009. He had a five-hour stopover. Some of his friends told him that he could have gotten a better connection than that, but he told them it was ok. That would make for the longest coffee in history! I marked the date on my calendar, asked if I could have the day off from work at the Lavender Farm, and then I told my mother. Well. She was about as excited as I was. She remembered Dave from his visit in 1975. (Do mothers ever forget anything?). And she actually put the date of our meeting on her calendar. She reminded me of how much he made me laugh.

In the interim, both of our other relationships had ended, and we started talking on the phone regularly. The friendship grew. Both Dave and I had injuries. I had cut my foot terribly and was on crutches, and Dave had put out his back. When July 23 arrived, I planned a picnic for us in Dorval on the shores of the Lake of Two Mountains. I packed chocolate, fruit, sandwiches, and some other treats in a big cooler and put it in the car along with my crutches and a couple of chairs. When we met at the airport, there were bear hugs and smiles on both our parts and maybe a hint of anticipation. We headed down to the aforementioned park, Gimpy and Gumpy, and sat there for hours, talking, reminiscing, and discovering. Oh, and we ate a little as well. That's not all we did…We shared our first kiss! That was the shortest but most amazing visit!   After Dave left for Calgary, we were both left alone to figure out what all had just happened. When he got back home to Nova Scotia, he called to tell me that he had bought three airline tickets: one for him to come to Montreal for a week in August; one for me to go to Nova Scotia for a week in October; and one for him to come to Montreal for two weeks at Christmas. We were set!

When Dave came to Montreal that August, we had a wonderful time -- my son drove us all over Montreal: to the Jean Talon Market, Mount Royal, St. Joseph's Oratory, a great Indian restaurant, and we finished up at Universite de Montreal where he gave us a private piano concert.

Over the course of that week we visited, we talked and talked, and we realized that we were in love. Imagine falling in love with your best friend – that's what happened to us. We kept marveling at how we could finish each other's sentences; how the years had melted away and we were still as impressed with each other as we had been way back when, except now there was romance in the mix. On his last evening in Quebec, we went for a six-course gourmet meal at a little French restaurant in St Eustache. When Dave was paying the bill, the waitress made some comment to him about us. He told her he was going to marry me, but that I didn't know it yet.

In October I flew to Nova Scotia just in time for the Autumn Pumpkin Fest and I met some of Dave's people. He had invited about 12 of his close friends to the house to meet me on the Sunday of my visit. Talk about feeling like a bug under the microscope! I think I did ok. When everyone finally left, Dave was a little antsy; said he wanted to take me for a drive. I went along with his idea, even though it was cold, windy and starting to drizzle rain. He brought his camera.

We drove to a place called The Lookoff where we got out of the car to see the view. I kept saying, "It would really be beautiful if it was a nice day" and wondering what we were doing there. Then Dave said he wanted to get a picture, and so he went back to the car for the camera. I was thinking that a picture in the rain was better than no picture at all, notwithstanding the fact that it was starting to get dark. Next thing I knew, Dave was down on one knee asking me to marry him and presenting me a ring! I was so taken aback; this was so unexpected that all I could say was, "You're crazy!" And he said, "Yes, but will you marry me?" I said YES!

We decided to get married in Montreal when he came for Christmas, 2009. My sister generously offered her house for the wedding and reception, and she prepared a huge Lebanese feast for the guests. There was baklava, stuffed grape leaves, tabouli, hummus, fatayer, pita bread and the ultimate kibbe. I made my own wedding cake, the cherry pound cake that my family is known for.

My parents were there, as well as Dave's sister and brother. My old friend Jenny was there too; she was the one who had been talking to Dave about me and me about Dave all that time. The air was festive, happy, joyous, and carefree, so different from my previous life. Can you guess what I gave each attendee as a little gift? A little pan of Divorce Fudge with a bag of lavender attached.

32
When the time is right

Cautiously, I put my house on the market. Again. All I could think of was how there were no offers the year before when I was planning to move to North Carolina. It was summertime and I was able to show the house in all its glory. I just couldn't understand why it didn't sell, but in the end it turned out to be a good thing when I called that relationship off. Where would I have lived if the house had sold?

I called the same real estate agent that I had the year before, Martin B. I think he was a little miffed when I took the house off the market before the contract was up, but I assured him that should I put it for sale in the future I would call him. He still had the listing in his file and wasted no time in making it active again. Once the sign went up in the front yard, all the naysayers came out of the woods. They told me I would never sell my house in the middle of winter. Some said it wouldn't sell because highway 640 ran right behind it, making a lot of noise. I figured that since the windows would be shut in the winter, visitors might not hear the sound. After the naysayers came the house of plagues. First there were ants in the cupboards. Big ones. I cleaned everything and put in the necessary ant poison. It took a while, but they were finally gone. After that came the mice. I had noticed lavender buds by the garbage in the kitchen, probably from decorating a batch of Divorce Fudge for the lavender shop. But alas, they weren't lavender buds. I knew I needed glasses, but this was getting ridiculous. Someone suggested I put a piece of cheese beside the garbage and if it was gone in the morning, it definitely wasn't lavender. Before I left for Nova Scotia, I had caught seven mice, and I hoped that would be the end of my problems.

It was almost Christmas and one day I noticed my cat was interested in something going on in a corner of the living room. She was looking up at the ceiling and then down at a flower arrangement on the floor. Drip, drip, drip. There was a leak, and when I pushed a broom handle to the ceiling, there was a gush of water. What next? Then came costly repairs to the leaking toilet upstairs, the repair and plastering of the ceiling, and finally a paint job. Who would buy a house with all those problems? I told myself that if its 'meant to be' the right buyer would come my way. I had a friend come to help me stage the house for the video that would be put up on the real estate site. I also learned how to stage it for prospective buyers. And then I waited. There were a few visitors to see the house in December that year, but only one offer that was too low to accept.

Christmas came, the wedding happened, and Dave went back to his job in Nova Scotia while I waited for my son's semester to end at the end of January. Surely the house would sell by then, wouldn't it?

The visits came to a grinding halt somewhere around the first week of January and I prepared to move to Nova Scotia while leaving an empty house. I got quotes from movers and chose one that took my freezer in exchange for all the boxes I would need for the move. I got a radio to leave on so that there would be sounds in the house. I arranged for snow clearing during my absence. Finally, I made arrangements with the insurance company who told me that the first month's insurance for an empty house would be the same as before, but after that it would rise substantially. The idea was that an empty house could garner problems that might not be caught in time. Another friend offered to do a walk through twice a week. So, it was all done, and the movers were coming on January 23rd. My plan was to follow them out of town.

As I sat in the window that January, looking out at the falling snow, the accumulating ice and the calendar dates marching onward toward the 23rd, I thought about my new life about to begin, and I despaired of ever selling the house. On the day before the movers were coming, we had a New Year's dinner at a local restaurant for the staff of Pure Lavande. My last hurrah, I thought. I wondered what the next day would bring, leaving my little cookie cutter house and heading to Nova Scotia, the movers, and my young son who was already starting to grieve leaving his friends and everything familiar. Literally, with my hand on the door to leave for the last supper with my lavender people, the phone rang. I felt a little irritated because I was already late but when I sat that it was Martin, my agent, I answered. He said that the people who had made the low-ball offer in December were back with a better offer, one that I accepted right away. Yes! They wanted to take possession of the house within two weeks. Yes! Martin said that he could come over right away for me to sign the papers because he knew that I was leaving town the next day.

I might have been a little late for the dinner that evening, but as I left the house for the second last time, Michelle's words rang in my ears, "It's not the right time to sell your house. When it's the right time, the buyer will come, and it will be easy."

It was the right time.

33

A New Life in Nova Scotia

I had thought that leaving Quebec and remarrying would heal me. You know, we always think, OK, if I just lose the weight or get the man or get that job or make this much money, all my bad feelings will go away. And they do go away for a while. But eventually you've got to get up in the morning and look in the mirror and acknowledge, 'Well, I'm still *me*.' The insecurities are still there. They're *inside*. It's not necessarily insecurity about the way I look; it's insecurity about my spirit and about who I am and about how I live my life.

I'll never forget driving with my young son to Nova Scotia and our new life and my new husband--as the miles melted away and Quebec was finally in the rear-view mirror, I started to feel a sense of freedom. As I drove through northern New Brunswick and continued south, memories of my past came in a flood. I remembered hitch hiking to St John with an old flame when I was a student at St FXU. I even chuckled to myself when I thought of one ride we had with a guy who was tired. He had been traveling for a long time because he was moving, and he was falling asleep. There was only one seat free in the car, so I had to sit on my boyfriend's lap and together we tried to keep this guy awake.

But when I crossed the border from New Brunswick into Nova Scotia, I felt like I was coming home – home to my new husband, my old university friend. Back home to where I used to be completely myself whether or not everyone liked it. I felt my moxie coming back and I started to sing. I had been given a second chance, a new start, an opportunity to put cults, religion and submission behind me. Little did I realize that I was still me with all my hangups, fears and preconceived beliefs about my role as a partner, a wife, and a human being in this world.

My happiness and optimism didn't last very long. After I had been settled in Nova Scotia for about five weeks it was my son's birthday, and as we were having the birthday meal at the table, the phone rang. I stood up to get it and saw on the call display that it was my ex, calling to wish his son Happy Birthday. I gave the phone to him and, without thinking about it, ran down to the bedroom where I curled up into a fetal position on the bed and started to shake. Dave realized there was something seriously wrong with me. Why did I do that, instinctively, without thinking about it? It was like a fight or flight feeling, and all of a sudden, I didn't feel safe anymore. I felt like I had to escape.

I wasn't sure at that point what I might have had to escape from. There was no one chasing me, no one holding me captive, no one forcing me to do things I didn't want to do, but the fear stayed. I needed to feel safe again. When I holed up in my office with the door shut, I felt a semblance of safety, but it was always short lived. I still felt that I had to look over my shoulder constantly. Eventually I realized that the fear I had was all coming from my own mind. In reality, I was in no danger, and I had nothing to fear. I needed to change my thought patterns and move forward. But I had no idea how to do that. Stuffing my feelings, fears and thought patterns to the back of my consciousness and pasting on that smile was never going to heal me from my former lifestyle.

After years of counseling and digging into my past I learned that my reaction that day was PTSD, Post Traumatic Stress Disorder. You don't get rid of that by moving to another province. In addition, I thought that all my problems stemmed from my marriage and divorce. It took a long time to understand that my ex was probably as brainwashed as I was, and that my issues came from distorted beliefs and a secluded lifestyle of fear and control.

You have to know the truth before you can attempt to heal from problems. I had been barking up the proverbial wrong tree for years before I understood that I had been in a cult. I spent hours in counseling with my pastor and also with several different licensed psychologists, but I was never able to explain to them what the real problem was. I talked about my first husband, my second husband, my divorce, and my loneliness, but I never told them I was in a cult. I didn't tell them because I didn't know.

34

A Paddle of Shame

After living in Nova Scotia with my son and new husband for a couple of years, the boxes were finally unpacked, and the house was put in order. It's not easy to merge two working households together. There were duplicates of many things, pots and pans, linens, gadgets, pillows, and the like. We had the task of deciding what would go and what would stay. Going through those boxes was painstaking. Which pictures should go on the wall? The ones from our respective pasts or some new ones that we might buy. And whose blankets should go on the master bed and which ones for the spare bed?

Among some old photographs and craft materials, I spied it. The dastardly paddle I had used on my children's tender bums during the cult years. At that stage of the game, it had been in disuse for several years. It was just a vestige from our past life. I had to chuckle when I saw it; I don't know why. To this day I have no idea why I felt it necessary to bring it, like a trophy, to my youngest son. Did I expect him to chuckle as well? With a grin on my face, I came up the stairs, paddle in hand and waved it at him. "Remember this?" As if he could forget.

And that's when my son proceeded to tell me all that the paddle represented for him. Pain, shame, never being able to please, not able to act like a child, and on it went. When he was done, I was white in the face, weak in the knees, and my heart was pounding. I told him I didn't realize how painful it was for him to be reminded of that part of his life. Once again, I told him I was sorry and asked for his forgiveness. I can tell you that I cried then. How could I have been so blind as to think he would have found the instrument of his pain and shame to be funny. I wondered when this mind of mine would ever make sense. I realized in that moment that in his eyes I was not a good mother, and that fact broke my heart. He had been angry for some time, and I could never figure out why. It wasn't just the paddle; it was also the whole ATI upbringing, he told me that day. Now it was time for some healing.

I said to him, "There is nothing I can do to change the past, but I want you to know how sorry I am for how I made you live. I was wrong. But you know that I am here for you now and I will always be here for you. I love you and I accept you. I have your back, no matter where you are or what you do. I love you."

That was the single most thing that restored my relationship with my son. I realized that we did need to move on and not live in the past, but first we need to understand what our past was, because we can't change it. And then we move on.

The discipline methods we had used came from a book called, <u>To Train Up a Child,</u> by Michael and Debi Pearl, who lived and homeschooled in the hills of Tennessee. It was a little book that they sold in bulk to people like me; homeschoolers and right-wing, patriarchal fundamentalists who were stern and joyless. I took the information in that book to heart because I believed it was how we were supposed to live, even if it was against what was in my heart. The book talked about when to spank, how to spank, where to spank and why to spank, all the while telling the child that you love him. Today those methods would be child abuse.

  That evening I went into the living room alone and burned the paddle in the fireplace, so sorry and ashamed of hurting my precious child. Later I told him about the burning and that I was glad he told me his truth about that paddle. Forgiveness is quite a powerful thing. When I expressed remorse and sadness and asked for forgiveness, it was the beginning of a long healing in our relationship.

  I confided to him that he was the main reason I didn't marry Don and move to North Carolina, and that unknowingly, he had saved my life. If I didn't have him to take care of, my dark thoughts during those days might have turned our lives into something tragic. He thanked me for the admission. Today he and I have a relationship that I could never have imagined a few years ago. It's a relationship of love, respect, and compassion, and understanding, as are my relationships with my other sons. In a way, if the paddle had to be the catalyst for us to make peace and have a great relationship, then it wasn't such a bad thing for me to bring it to his attention that day.

35
Finding out I Was in a Cult

2014 was a year to remember.

  As my mother lay in the hospital, dying of the cancer that ravaged her body, I made a discovery that once again changed my view of the world and my life. As I watched my mother's cancer take over her body and I wondered who I would be when she was no longer there, other forces were at work to change how I saw myself and my place in the world. My mother, my anchor, would be leaving us and then, as the oldest daughter of four, I would become the matriarch of the family.

  I tried hard to put my first marriage and the homeschooling years behind me. It wasn't always easy because I found that my way of thinking was quite different from everyone else's. I knew that being in ATI had changed me, but I really didn't realize to what extent. Most of the time I just thought that I had a different perspective than other people, even my family.

  I had flashbacks. Certain hymns we sang in my new church brought me back to my past lifestyle and all that I had lost. I would find myself crying and not able to sing at all. I don't think anyone noticed, and I used to return from church and feel depressed for several days. I wondered when I was going to be able to put it all behind me. Sometimes I longed for the safety of the isolation my family had in ATI.

But a few years ago, I did a series of blogs called "The Positively No Negativity Challenge". I purposed to write a blog entry every day for 84 days, and I succeeded. Each morning I got up at 5AM, reflected on the events of the past day or so, and began to write something positive. One day it would be about gratitude; another day I wrote about paying a compliment. Every day I published a blog, and as the days passed, I became happier because the more I wrote, the more positive I became. I gained many new followers on the blog, and it was exciting that they commented on what I had written. Some of them told me that they looked forward to my morning writing each day.

However, there did come a day when I was stumped about what to write. We had been having stormy winter weather that January in Nova Scotia and I hadn't been out for a couple of days. Since most of my positive blog entries came from encounters with people, I had no new experiences to write about. I started thinking about life, self-acceptance and what a hard time I had with accepting myself and my past. That got me to thinking about a song the children sang in the ATI Children's Programs. Yes, there was indoctrination for the children as well as the adults. But there was this song that taught about the ten unchangeables we all have in life. It was a cute song and outlined the things we cannot change.

1. Our uniqueness
2. Our parents
3. Our brothers and sisters
4. Our nationality
5. Our mental capacity
6. Our time in history
7. Whether we're male or female
8. Our birth order in the family
9. How we age
10. How and when we die

    I thought it would be a good topic for that day's blog post. Looking back, that day was a turning point in my evolution as a human being and in understanding that I had more to heal from than just my divorce. As I listened to that song on YouTube, it brought me back to when my children were young, how we lived and how that lifestyle made me feel.
    I searched for more children's songs from ATI. The more I found, the more distressed I became until my internet searches caused me to stumble on a site called Recovering Grace. I started reading.
    Recovering grace (https://www.recoveringgrace.org) is a site dedicated to helping the ATI generation find healing from the teachings of the Advanced Training Institute. Intrigued, since my whole Christian experience was through these teachings, I started reading the articles on the site. Most of them were written by people who had been raised in ATI which was now being called a cult.

I had never considered that I had been in a cult and had raised my children in one. I remembered Bill Gothard's teaching on cults and being taught on how to respond to our critics who might say that ATI was a cult. Surely it wasn't.

But looking back, I realized that ATI fit the definition of a cult that we had been taught. We had learned that cults were secretive. We were secretive, having been told to never lend or share our materials with non-ATI people. We had been instructed to smile all the time even when we were sad. We also had been told to 'never give a bad report', meaning that we could never speak negatively about what was going on at home, either about our spouses or our lifestyle, a concept that concealed a lot of abuse and hardship in families. Women were not allowed to look sad because it would be a reflection on their husbands, a public rebuke as we were told.

But we all had things to be sad and anxious about. Everyone does, at one time or another. I had just never thought about that before. And when you investigate what cults are and what they do, we surely were it. We were defined by our unusual religious and spiritual beliefs. We had a common interest in following our leader. We had goals and mannerisms that isolated us from the rest of the world. Some people define a cult as a group that uses undue influence to create obedience and dependency.

Steven Hassan, a licensed mental health professional and one of the leading experts on cults had this to say about cult behavior.

> *"You can't be angry, you can't talk about what's going on, you can't review this kind of spirituality because in so doing, you are not being spiritual. Not only can you not be angry, but you also can't gossip and you have to forgive. But some things are unforgivable. That makes a perfect set up for abuse and control."*

    I literally ate up that little site called Recovering Grace. I bookmarked it so that I wouldn't miss any new articles, and new ones were being written every day. The more I read, the more the door to my past opened. A flood of memories, most of them not wonderful, came into my consciousness. I started to realize that after ten years out of ATI, most of my hang-ups, much of my reluctance to get involved with other people and organizations, and all of my personal baggage came from being involved in this cult. And I had thought it was because of my divorce. Around that time, I stopped blaming my ex for all the difficulties in my life as I realized that we both had been totally brainwashed.

    I was in shock over everything that had been exposed on the Recovering Grace website. Through the articles as well as the Parents Recovering Grace page on Facebook, I came to realize that the sexual abuse and manipulation from my ex was only a fraction of what had happened to me and by consequence, shaped my thought patterns for over 25 years.

    I realized that I had been spiritually abused. Meaning that the scriptures were so twisted in our teachings that my understanding was totally false. I finally understood why I always felt shame and unworthiness in my first marriage, and why it spilled over into my second marriage

I always thought that the good things in life and love were for other people; people who deserved them. Not for me, because I was a lousy lover, at least that's what my ex always said. I could never please him. He was insatiable. So, I never felt like a good wife.

  I had a hard time to understand that I had been abused emotionally. He always used a nice tone of voice, but the damage was the same as if the words were physical blows. He never raised his voice to me, never raised a hand to me, and yet he broke my spirit so badly that I became completely numb inside.

  I used to wonder how I could get away from him. I would never have left my children, so it was never an option. But sometimes I imagined being so sick that I wouldn't be able to have sex with him. Most of the time I would rather have been dead.

  The Recovering Grace site was created to help young adults who had been raised in ATI to shine a light on what had happened to them and to share their stories. I had not been raised in it; I did the raising and was now finally understanding the magnitude of giving my children that kind of rigid upbringing. Sometimes I have a hard time to believe that they still love me, but they do.

  A spinoff of Recovering Grace was a Facebook page called ATI Parent Recovery Group. I quickly joined and introduced myself:

"Hello and thank you for the add. I am happy to have found Recovering Grace recently as I have been quite silent on my fourteen years as an ATI mom. I got out when my husband left me for another woman, and I put my youngest son in school for the first time, in grade five. My older sons had already gone on to university. I had a very difficult time to find my place in the world after my divorce; I didn't know how to dress, what music to listen to, how to raise my son alone and I was afraid of everything outside my kitchen window, thinking that the whole world was evil. Thankfully I am doing better now and have remarried to a man who is trying hard to understand me. I realize now that I am in recovery and am still dealing with the misinformation and hurts of my time in ATI. Thank you all so much for reading."

I was thankful for that Facebook page. Every day I read, posted and responded to other men and women who like me, were trying to dismantle their unhealthy thought patterns and to learn how to differentiate between true and false teachings. We compared notes. I remembered being told time after time at the seminars and in the schoolwork that we had to 'die to self', and one day I asked in the group, "Did you ever get so tired of being told to 'die to self'? Some answers:

(Names have been changed)

Cathy: "Yes."

Sonia: "Especially when it felt like I was the only one who was dying to self."

Mary: "Why did God make me if I wasn't supposed to be myself?"

Judy: "If you die to self long enough, you just might die."

Clarissa: "I got tired of being told to do things that I really didn't know how to do and when I tried to learn, nobody could really explain."

Gary: "As a man I was so tired of doing things this way and only this way. It helped destroy my marriage. We were involved with one family and if I wasn't like them, we weren't accepted."

Debra: "I spent my whole life trying to get people to love me for me."

Dominic: "Scripture never says we are to die to self. It says that the person who wants to follow Christ should DENY himself and take up the cross…and if dying to self were so great, wouldn't suicide be the ultimate spiritual act? One of the things that opens a person to abuse and depersonalization is the loss of self in a relationship. God doesn't want us to come as 'dead meat'. He wants us as he created us – with wonder, love, joy, grace, creativity, freedom and so much more."

The ATI Parent Recovery Group became my lifeline. Every day I learned and became more aware of what had happened to me. Finally, I was in a place where people had lived the exact same thing I had lived, and they felt exactly the same as I did. I had never talked about my cult experience for two reasons: first of all, I never understood that ATI was a cult and that there was anything wrong with it and secondly, I had been so well taught to never give a bad report, and I never did.

Since most of ATI families were from the US, when I moved to Nova Scotia, I never met another family who knew about ATI and no one in NS had ever heard about Bill Gothard, the Basic Seminar nor the Advanced Training Institute. Once I learned the truth of what had happened to me, I started talking. My new husband could only listen because there was absolutely nothing in his life that could relate to what I was telling him. I became the verbal diarrhea woman, and I didn't stop talking for two years. I talked so much not only to tell others what I had lived but also to try to remember and to understand myself.

36

The Dawning of Understanding

Once I had found the Recovering Grace site, I finally understood a lot of things about myself. First, since ATI was so male dominant, and women were to be submissive and protected by their husbands, it made me feel that I was a nobody without a husband. I would never have told my children that my full-time job was to find a new husband. I wish I could have had the chance to be who I was and to be happy with who I was without yearning for a husband. Also, if I had lived in an English place, would I have been able to be happy alone?

I think so…maybe.

I was in shock over everything that was exposed on the Recovering Grace website. Through the articles as well as the Parents page on Facebook, I came to realize that male headship and patriarchy were only a fraction of what happened to me and by consequence shaped my thought patterns for most of my adult life. Many of the people in that parent's group had also been divorced. It's hard for a marriage to survive that kind of lifestyle.

I used to think that I could never measure up, no

matter how hard I tried. I never thought that I was enough just as I was. I was constantly waiting for a change in myself that never happened. I remember crying out to God to change me. But he never did. I always thought that the good things in life and love were for other people; people who deserved them. Not for me, because I was lacking somehow. During the time in the cult my spirit was broken so badly that I became completely numb inside.

    I often wondered how I could escape. I used to ask my husband to please let me go to a hotel for a couple of nights with some knitting and a couple of books, just to get a break and to be alone long enough to have a complete thought, but I was never allowed.

    I learned about spiritual manipulation. Thinking always that God's love, my husband's love, my parent's love, anyone's love was contingent on my performance. I could never measure up to what I perceived everyone expected of me. In my eyes everyone was disappointed in me.

    My husband was disappointed in me because I was not able to measure up in certain ways for him. My parents were disappointed in me because I was living a life so separate from how they raised me and as much as they tried, they never understood what we were doing to ourselves and our children. I was disappointed in myself because I was supposed to be happy and content, but I was not. I kept feeling that I was doing something wrong and if only I could figure out what that was, I could fix it and be happy.

There were so many more 'principles'. The teachings we adhered to have broken up families and relationships. The guiding principle of 'turning the hearts of the children to their fathers and the hearts of the fathers to their children' has really resulted in the opposite, as many children, as soon as they were able, left home and many don't speak to their parents anymore.

Once I had learned the truth, I tried to protect myself and to come out of all this with grace. (What we had learned about grace was false also). I couldn't pretend any more that what we did was good and right, although I know I did it with a sincere heart and I'm happy that my children have been able to forgive me for the way of life that was imposed on them. My youngest son forgave me, after years of anger. I finally have my son back, no thanks to the Advanced Training Institute.

I think my mother wanted to be proud of me for the most part, but when you're not proud of yourself you don't see yourself as others do. I wanted to be enough just as I was, but my mother always introduced me with qualifications.

When I was a student: "This is my daughter Christine. She is studying at ST FXU.

When I taught school: "This is my daughter Christine. She is teaching in Alberta."

When I married my first husband: "This is my daughter Christine. She is married to a Chiropractor."

When I got divorced: "This is my daughter Christine."

Finally.

I now have a new title: Cult survivor. You may think that's not something to be proud of, but it did help me to redefine and understand myself, and I'm proud of that.

Then I had to deal with the fallout from ATI and the lies we believed. I hated the fact that I let myself get into such a cult. I can't believe that I wore those long dresses and liked it. And the stupid things we used to say all the time like, "Others may, you may not" or "We have a sin nature.".

I think we fooled ourselves. Everyone else just went on with their lives and probably pitied us. For the record, I pity who we were. I wondered why I followed my husband around for 21 years, never really questioning, just crying because I couldn't do it all. Sometimes I feel that I lost those years of my life when I could have been enjoying my kids so much more, and at the same time, developing my own interests. Why did I have to live that life? And then I couldn't leave because I had three children who needed me, and besides, I had no money or skills to do much of anything. I could only dream of having a place to myself where I could daydream, do crafts, read and knit. I have that now, but I am a senior citizen. I mourn the time lost with my children when they were young. But they don't mourn because living the way we did was the only way they knew how to live at the time. When they matured and left home they found a whole new world out there and they embraced it.

I recently read something about only feeling loved when you are doing things for the people you love and if you stop doing, calling, suggesting, sending cards and gifts and initiating, that the person would not love you anymore. Sometimes I absolutely felt that way. I didn't feel loved just because of who I was, but because of what I did or didn't do.

Why couldn't I just have been me?
What would my life look like if I just let it happen? Would I be loved more? Less? Not at all?

In my first marriage perfection was key. I never felt that I measured up, never felt that I was good enough no matter how hard I tried. That has carried over to all parts of my life. One day Dave was saying that I don't see myself as other people see me. I see a person with no confidence who can't get people to read her blog, who still tries to sell stuff at craft shows and feels second rate when things don't sell. I see someone who gets sick to her stomach when she's asked to do something that puts her in the spotlight.

Then Dave told me how others see me. They see a woman of courage who has overcome much. They see someone who has written and self-published a book, is somewhat of an expert on Lavender growing and usage. People also see me as a compassionate woman whose wisdom has helped them along the way.

37

I Can See Clearly Now

It has been a few years since I lived in the confines of the ATI cult in St Eustache, Quebec, and it's taken a long time for me to realize that who I am is not only important but it's vital to understanding myself and my place in the world. Gone are the days of living, dressing, and behaving according to a list of rules and regulations that governed how I related to my husband, my children, and the people around me.

      It comforts me to see how I've changed in my attitudes, my self-acceptance and how I am able to see my value as a person. At this stage of my life, I am a senior and it does me good to look back at how I was during the cult years and see how I've evolved into a whole person since that time. It's incredible when I think of it, how the cult principles, practices, attitudes, and beliefs took over my way of thinking and made me into a different person. Sometimes now when I sit down and take stock of what I believed then compared to now, I find it heart wrenching to understand who I was back then. My family, my children and people who have known me most of my life have seen the difference and have often exclaimed, "Thank God you're back!" Because really, they had lost me inasmuch as I had lost myself and my way. I would like to think that I am a better person now, a more compassionate and loving woman because of what I have gone through. I've written down some of the many false beliefs I had during the cult years and what I believe now. Sometimes it's a good thing to write them down so that I can see from how far I've come in my evolution as a human being in this world.

I used to think that I needed a strong-minded man to lead me and tell me what to do. Now I know that I don't need to be led. I can make my own decisions.

I used to be afraid to express an opinion, because what I said might contradict what my husband would say. Now I express myself because I am an individual with my own thoughts and opinions.

I used to find my value in who my family was, what my husband did and how well I followed a prescribed set of rules and regulations.
Now I find my value in who I am, what I like, and how I relate to the world.

I used to think that dressing modestly meant wearing long dresses and not showing any flesh, like wearing sleeveless tops, skirt slits and a vee neck t-shirt.
Now I know that to be modest is more of an attitude than of covering flesh. There is a world of difference between dressing like a nun and dressing like a woman.

I used to believe that my life was to be spent in service to my family and that I had to die to my own interests and aptitudes.

I've since learned that pursuing my interests, like writing, quilting, rug hooking, knitting and being outdoors are important to my own well-being and that makes me a better wife, mother and friend.

While I was in the cult of ATI, I thought that I was an incapable person, not worthy of love and happiness because I couldn't measure up, no matter how hard I tried; with homeschooling, with my husband, with my extended family and with myself. I realized much later, years in fact, that I had disconnected from who I was and what I loved in order to survive. I know now that I am worthy of every good thing and that my voice counts.

When my husband left, I told my children that my full-time job was to find another husband because I didn't think I could survive without a man at my side I've since proven that I am a survivor, that I can do pretty much anything I set my mind to, and that no partner at all is much better than the wrong partner.

I used to think that being a single woman was a mark of disgrace and shame. I thought that somehow an unmarried woman had brought it on herself, whether she had been divorced or never married. When I became a single mom, I realized that everyone's story is different and I learned to have compassion and love for women who were alone, for whatever reason.

I used to think that children should be seen and not heard, that they should conform to someone else's idea of who they should be.

Nowadays I love to watch my children grow into responsible adults, trying one thing and then another, making mistakes and learning from them. I don't think children should ever be insulated from making mistakes.

I used to think that I had to earn love by being someone that I am not or doing things that I really don't want to do.

I have finally concluded that if someone doesn't like me the way I am, it's not my problem. I cannot please everyone all of the time, and I'm at peace with that.

I always thought we were put here on the earth to serve God, and if that included hardship, then so be it.

Now I know that God put us here to laugh and enjoy our lives and to be happy. He didn't put us here to be sad and eat prunes and all bran all day because we were constipated both in body and in spirit.

I used to think that divorce would be the absolutely worst thing that could happen to me and that it would make God angry.

I know now that the worst thing is to live an unhappy life with someone who is unsuitable for me, and that not only God, but also my friends and family want to see me happy and safe.

When I was in ATI, I thought that rock music in any form was evil. If the music made a person want to dance and tap their toes, it was wrong.

These days I listen to many different kinds of music, and I love to dance and tap my toes. It's an expression of joy and lightheartedness, not to mention an expression of personality.

Back in the day, I stopped listening to the news and reading the newspaper because it made me fearful. I thought that I should insulate myself from all the bad things in the world.

Now I think that someone who chooses to avoid the news misses out on opportunities to help others and becomes an uninformed person.

It's taken me a long time to figure out who I've been all along. Working through and overcoming my traumas ignited my resilience and lit a fire of sacred purpose in my soul. When I saw how hurtful the world can be, I also see the many ways I can make a difference.

In the heart of my suffering there is a calling to help heal others who have walked a similar path. It is only now as I begin to write about my experience, that I can understand what happened to me and my family over the 14 years we were 100% involved in the Advanced Training Institute.

There is a scripture that talks about a 'holy generation, set apart for God's glory. 1 Peter 2:9- "But you are a chosen people, a royal priesthood a holy nation, God's special possession, that you may declare the praises of him who called you out of darkness into his wonderful light."

We 'knew' that we were the chosen people in that verse, and warnings from friends and family fell on deaf ears.

38

Three Questions

There are three questions that beg to be asked. The first one is, "what was the attraction of the cult?

I think that as a newly born-again Christian, I wanted to know as much as I could about how to rightly live the Christian life, both outwardly and inwardly. I was also attracted to the uniqueness and protection that I perceived ATI would offer me. They had rules and lists for every aspect of life, so participating in it was sort of like a guidebook for living the best way. If we had a health, discipline, clothing, relationship or any other kind of issue, there were answers within the cult. Husbands were even told to give their wives direct access to them at work. So anytime I needed to talk to my husband, I'd call the office and the secretary had been instructed to pass the phone over to him right away, no questions asked. You could say, it was cloistered but it was cozy. I knew that my marriage, my children and my life were protected, and there's a lot of solace in that.

The next thing people wonder is, why did I give up all my power in following the cult rules and submitting to my husband in all things. I had been an independent-spirited type of person all my life and now I was going around in a long dress and trying to emulate a 'meek and quiet' spirit. It's sort of like the frog in the boiling water story; I loved the framework of my life at first but as the years went on, I realized that I had indeed given up my power. Not only that, but I had also given up my personality, my desires and my laughter. It happened slowly at first, and there were good explanations for each thing we did, backed up by scripture. By the time I realized that I was a completely different person from what my prior friends and my family knew, I was so entrenched in the cult that I didn't know how to assert myself and be myself. Heck, I didn't even know who I was anymore, nor what I wanted.

Lastly, no one around me could understand what I thought was promised to me by following all the rules of the cult. I remember one day at church when another couple was interested in our way of life and wanted to know more. I'll never forget the father saying to us, "I want to do everything I can to be the best father I can be." I guess we felt the same. We were repeatedly taught that if we follow God's word (as taught to us by him), God would 'turn the hearts of the fathers to the children and he would also turn the hearts of the children to the fathers.' And that our children would 'stand before kings'. That's quite a promise. We worked hard to make all that happen. Sadly, a lot of young people, when they had graduated from homeschool high school, left home and left all the cult rules and regulations behind. Many of them became alienated from their parents for many years.

What I changed because of learning from my past mistakes in ATI:

- I learned to believe my son when he told me something rather than always being suspicious and thinking he was 'up to something'. This was huge in developing my relationship with him.
- I learned to not judge my adult children, nor to give them unsolicited advice; rather, if they discuss a problem with me, I tell them what worked for me and that maybe the same might work for them.
- I learned to turn a blind eye when my young adult children did things I did not approve of. I let them make their own mistakes.
- I learned to be more assertive with my second husband (not ATI) and that marriage (for us anyway) is not only a two-way street but also an equal partnership where we both make decisions.
- I learned to not be a doormat for anyone, ever.
- I'm sorry, but I do not 'reverence' my husband; I always hated that word. However, I do love him and respect him. Big difference to me.
- I've learned that children are to be loved and allowed to develop as they will, rather than fitting some mold that I or someone else thinks they should fit.
- I learned to embrace the differences in each of my family members, and to accept them.
- Divorce humbled me. I no longer judge divorced people, single mothers or people who choose an alternative

- lifestyle as I used to, thinking somehow that their state was their own fault.
- I let my children see my weaknesses rather than letting them continue to think that I am perfect, stoic, and unfeeling.
- I am not afraid to admit to my own weakness and imperfection. In fact, I like my imperfections.

It's often easy to blame all the negatives in your life on someone else. Most often people blame their parents for their lack of success, their troubles, their fears, not being able to keep a job and all sorts of things that are not working in their lives. Sometimes they're right, and sometimes they are not. Overcoming the past can be a lifelong journey. Other people blame their spouse, their ex or their boss. After all, if we have someone to blame, we never have to take responsibility for the things that are wrong in our lives.

For many years I blamed my ex for my lack of confidence, my digestive issues, and the fact that I was afraid of many things. I blamed him because I had financial issues, I blamed him for my loneliness, and I blamed him for overpowering me and manipulating me. I was the victim, even if he told me many times there are no victims. I still felt like one.

39

Out Of the Ashes, Beauty Will Rise

People who knew me during the cult years and who are still a part of my life are amazed that I've come through the fire that was cult living. Some people say I'm brave; others say I have a lot of fortitude and yet others are proud of me and how I came through without bitterness and anger, even if I do have some regrets. When certain close friends and family members knew the true story of my life, the story I had kept hidden, they have said things like, I didn't know; you've had a difficult time of it. It was very, very hard, and you didn't deserve that. You're stronger than any person I've ever met. You don't deserve what you went through.

I might not have deserved what I went through, but I've always been a person who sees the lighter side of life and tries to find the good in things that are not good. As much as they were difficult years, it wasn't all bad. I know that what I went through helped me to become a better person and mother than before.

My children learned how to run a house. These days, that is pure gold. They know how to make bread, and I've shared the recipe with you in the Appendix. My boys can clean a bathroom thoroughly. In fact, I remember teaching them how to clean the toilet and the older boys fighting over who would get to use the Fantastic Cleanser Spray.

My children know how to budget their money, even if

they don't always do it. They know how to save and make good financial decisions. They know why it's a good idea to pay down debt quickly because of all the interest paid over the long term. All this was taught through the Financial Freedom seminars, and it became a part of our lives. To this day my husband and I have a pouch that is divided into sections for groceries, medical, restaurant, church, etc. The money is put in each section at the beginning of the month and is a good way to gauge where we are at any given time.

I learned how to be money savvy – in fact, I don't think I have ever made a bad financial decision.

I can now spot a dangerous cult a mile away. Once there was a family that came to our church (post cult) and they performed in song and dance for us. To the average onlooker, they were a cute family with a devout performance. As for me, I could see the little nuances of submission in their eyes and body language, and it troubled me. I spoke to my pastor later about it and mentioned that I was uncomfortable, not with their beautiful performance, but about the other things that were going on. He told me that he also had gotten a bad feeling about them from the way they related to each other, how after the service, each word was measured, and they had a hard time to look you in the eye. You could say I had developed a certain kind of discernment and it has served me well these past few years.

One thing I know for sure is that my time in ATI and the years that followed have taught me to be a much more compassionate person, more loving, more tolerant, and more able to experience joy and to have fun. I had been on the dark side. Now I am in the Light.

My feelings on ATI, looking back:
Not too long ago, my son showed me several home videos taken while we were in ATI. They were mostly taken on Christmas mornings over the years as we opened gifts around the Christmas tree with my parents-in-law present. And before that, a friend showed me some videos of me and my family at a 50th birthday party for her husband. I don't know what my son or my friend saw in those movies, but it took me a couple of years to consent to watch the Christmas ones.

While my son was having a good laugh at how we used to be, I was crying. I looked at myself and saw a beautiful woman who was squashed and constantly told she was not good enough. I saw a woman with no self-confidence who should have had self-confidence. I saw a woman who was living what many Christian women are living now: obliged to have sex no matter how she was feeling and taking home pregnancy tests regularly in her 50s. She remained quiet rather than pointing out error in what was being taught. I saw children who were cookie cutter images of all the other ATI children, rattling off the right responses and wearing the right clothes but dying inside.

I went through a process of disassembling all those misconceptions, which helped me to overcome things I thought were just a part of my being. These are very important issues. I feel that now, several years out of the cult and my crazy marriage, I can relate to the world like a normal person. I see men as equals, not as people who are more important than me and who can control my life.

I've learned that because of my past life I have become a woman who is more compassionate, more discerning, gracious, forgiving, and most definitely stronger. You could say that I've been humbled and compensated for the grief, shame, loneliness and self-doubt that I experienced while in ATI and the years following when I didn't know who I was anymore.

Below is a little essay by Emerson. I ran across it while I was struggling with the pain and hopelessness in my life that came from being in a cult, my divorce, and the agony of wondering what was left of my life when my marriage and lifestyle ended at age fifty-one. When I read it, it touched me deeply, and it still does. I felt it to be extremely profound, as if it were written just for me. In the essay, Emerson lists calamities that are unpaid losses, and you may well add divorce, because it is one of life's most painful losses.

Concerning his speaking of death, you would do well to consider and accept that divorce is also a death - the death of a marriage and of a way of life. In this essay, I hear Emerson telling me that, not in spite of, but because of the tragedies that may befall us during our lifetimes, these tragedies can bring about changes in our lives which could ruin us, but which, instead, give us the chance to change and grow into a much stronger person who can be of much more value to mankind.

This essay is one of my most favorite pieces of

literature. It means so very much to me, and I hope that you will understand any calamity that you have gone through a little better after reading it.

Compensation
By Ralph Waldo Emerson

The compensations of calamity are made apparent
to the understanding also, after long intervals of time.
A fever, a mutilation, a cruel disappointment, a loss of wealth,
a loss of friends, seems at the moment
unpaid loss, and unpayable. But the sure years reveal
the deep remedial force that underlies all facts.
The death of a dear friend, wife, brother, lover,
which seemed nothing but privation, somewhat
later assumes the aspect of a guide of genius;
for it commonly operates revolutions in
our way of life, terminates an epoch of infancy or of youth,
which was waiting to be closed, breaks up a wonted occupation,
or a household, of style of living, and allows the formation
of new ones more friendly to the growth of character. It
permits or constrains the formation of new acquaintances
and the reception of new influences that prove
of the first importance to the next years,
and the man or woman who would have remained a
sunny garden flower, with no room for its roots and too
much sunshine for its head, by the falling of the walls

and the neglect of the gardener is made the Banyan of the forest,
yielding shade and fruit to wide neighborhoods of men.

    When I first read this essay, I understood it and it gave me some comfort. When I read it over and over, I gained a new understanding of what had happened to me. But when I learned a few things about the Banyan tree, my understanding went to a whole new level, and I realized that this was not only a powerful piece of literature but something that had profound meaning for my life.
    I learned that the banyan tree grows throughout Cambodia and some other countries. It may reach a height of over 100 feet, and as it grows, new roots descend from its branches, pushing into the ground and forming new trunks. A single banyan tree might have dozens of trunks, and it is often impossible to tell which is the original.
    At this stage of my life, I can say that there have been compensations along my journey to healing. I've made friends I never would have made during the cult years. I've also been able to help other people who were suffering along the way, because now I have compassion for them, whereas before I would have judged them. And finally, after all these years, the walls of shame and obligations have fallen and have given rise to a new life of grace, mercy and freedom.
    I'm not so sure I'll ever be a banyan tree. I'd settle for being a red maple. They offer cover and shade for the weary, and they're not too complicated.

In my office there is a framed print that I hung in 2014. It was designed by a woman from a Southern state who knew and understood the bondage and shame of living under ATI rules. I leave it there as a reminder of what my mindset was then, and what it is now. It says:

She had not known the grace until she felt the freedom

Book club discussion questions

Many thanks to "Between the Covers", a lively book club in Corner Brook, Newfoundland, for the insightful questions for discussion.

1. Why do you think it took Christine so long to realize she was in a cult, despite all the characteristics of a cult that she was living every day?

2. What cult behaviours were prevalent in the life that Christine adhered to?

3. What double standards were present in the Advanced Training Institute?

4. The Advanced Training Institute (ATI) appeared to be the guiding factor in establishing the cult behaviour. Why do you think the people were so receptive to the teachings of the Institute?

5. What do you think of the education curriculum for children in the cult? i.e. the scholarly Wisdom Booklets based on the Sermon on the Mount. How did this curriculum prepare the children for further education?

6. What effect do you think living in a cult and being educated by ATI standards had on the children? Did they miss out on the mystery and wonder of childhood? i.e. no Christmas or Halloween traditions, no socialization outside the cult.

7. Obviously living in a cult took an emotional toll on Christine, leading to depression. A therapist helped her realize

that she was also suffering from PTSD. What factors in her cult life contributed to this?

8.   After her divorce and leaving the cult, Christine set out to redefine herself. She had great difficulty with this. Her belief that she needed a husband hindered her ability to move on independently. Why did she hold this belief and what other beliefs from ATI affected her ability to find herself?

9.   Do you feel that Christine has finally found herself? What evidence supports your answer?

Appendix

On breadmaking:

One very important thing is to add ascorbic acid to the mix. Ascorbic acid is just plain old vitamin C. I crush two 500 mg vitamin C tablets and add it when adding the flour. This makes bread that is spongier and less crumbly. The sweetener is what makes the yeast work and gives well-risen bread. So you can't have completely sweetener-free bread. I have used everything from maple syrup to honey, white sugar, brown sugar and molasses, all with good results.

Did you know that too much flour in the mix could make bread that is tough and dry? Most people add too much flour while kneading it on the counter so that the dough doesn't stick. I oil the counter with a little of the oil from the recipe. It works great. So, if the recipe calls for 1/2 cup of oil, I'll put most of it in the mix, but save some for the kneading. I oil the counter as well as my hands. Nothing sticks! And the bread doesn't come out dry and cracked. Here is the recipe I developed:

Excellent Whole Wheat Bread

3 cups warm water (45 deg C)

2/3 cup white sugar
2 Tbsp active dry yeast
1 1/2 tsp salt 1 500 mg tablet of vitamin C, crushed with the back of a spoon

1/3 cup oil
6 cups whole-wheat flour
2 cups white flour

In a large bowl, dissolve the sugar in the warm water and then stir in the yeast. Allow proofing until the mixture resembles creamy foam, about 10 minutes. Mix salt and most of the oil into the yeast mixture. Mix in the vitamin C and the flour, one cup at a time. Knead dough on a slightly oiled surface for about 10 minutes or until the dough becomes elastic.

Place the dough in a well-oiled bowl, cover and let rise in a warm place until doubled in bulk, about one hour. I find that the top of the fridge is a nice warm spot. Punch the dough down. Knead about 10 times and divide into three loaves. Place into three well-oiled loaf pans, cover and let rise for 30 minutes or until dough has risen about one inch above the pans. Bake in a preheated 350-degree oven for 35 minutes. Let cool on racks before bagging. Makes 3 loaves

Divorce Fudge*

3 cups brown sugar
5 oz carnation milk
1/2 lb butter
2 cups icing sugar

Combine brown sugar, milk and butter in a pot. Over a medium heat, bring it to the boil, stirring. Once it boils, lower the heat and put the timer on for 4 minutes, stirring occasionally. Remove from heat. With the beaters running, slowly add in the icing sugar until the mixture is smooth. Pour into a greased 9 X 13 pan and let cool overnight. Cut into squares.

*The fudge does not cause divorce and you don't have to be divorced to enjoy some.

Scripturewear Brooch:

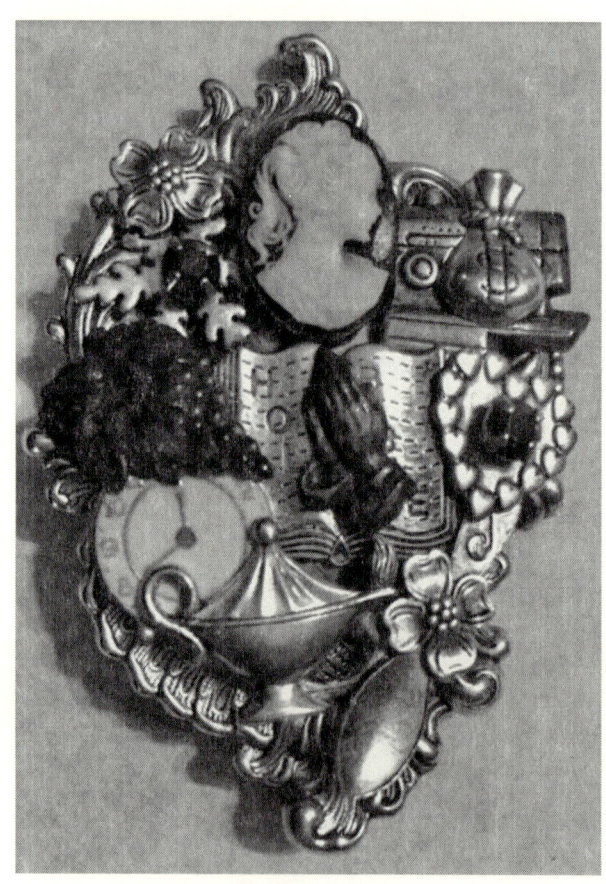

Afterword

It has been many years since I've been out of ATI and after all this time, my life is still affected by the cult. It has been a process of de-programming myself day after day. There is really no counselor or psychologist, not even a pastor where I live, who is able to begin to understand what I went through in ATI. I've had to counsel myself and commune with my new friends on the ATI Parent Recovery Group on Facebook. They really know what went on.

I still went to see psychologists in an effort to understand myself. The first one who told me I had PTSD helped me to understand, just a little, that what I went through was not normal. I have triggers which I'll probably take to the grave. One is dresses and another is hymns. There are certain kinds of loose dresses that I'm not able to wear and when I see them on a store rack, I get a sick feeling in my gut. When I'm at church and they play a familiar hymn, like "When We See Christ", or "Trust and Obey", or "What a Friend we have in Jesus", it brings me right back to ATI conferences and all the hardship, shame and unworthiness I felt back then.

In 2014 Bill Gothard, 80 at the time, was forced out of the organization over allegations that he abused young women working at ATI Headquarters.

ATI's poster family, the Duggars of 19 Kids and Counting ended up having their show cancelled in 2015 amid revelations that their oldest son molested four of his sisters as a young teen. As if that wasn't enough, in late 2021 the same Josh Duggar, now 33, was convicted of downloading and possessing child sex abuse images on his work computer. On May 25, 2022, Josh Duggar was sentenced to 12.5 years in prison for possession of child pornography. Imagine, every time someone looks at that child porn, those children are re-abused. A history professor at Baylor University, said Gothard's fundamentalist patriarchal teachings help create environments where abuse is more likely to go unchecked.

She said, "As men, they have more authority than women, their voice counts more, and women have this propensity to be valued more for their sexual role, so it allows abuse to flourish."

christinefaour@gmail.com

Manufactured by Amazon.ca
Acheson, AB